THE
DOLLHOUSE
SOURCEBOOK

THE DOLLHOUSE SOURCEBOOK

Caroline Clifton-Mogg
Principal photography by Nick Nicholson

Abbeville Press   Publishers
New York   London   Paris

First published in the United States of America in 1993
by Abbeville Press, 488 Madison Avenue,
New York, NY 10022

First published in United Kingdom in 1993
by Cassell plc, Villiers House, 41/47 Strand,
London WC2N 5JE, U.K.

ISBN 1-55859-613-5

Edited and designed by Toucan Books Limited, London

Printed and bound in Italy

Jacket photographs:
Front: Interior from miniature Palace of Versailles,
by Kevin Mulvany and Susan Rogers.
Back: *TL* Miniature tableware from Museum of Childhood, Bethnal Green, London,
by courtesy of the Board of Trustees of the Victoria and Albert Museum, London;
TR/BL/BR Bernard Hall by Paul Wood, on show
at the London Toy and Model Museum.

Page 1: The hall of the oldest known baby house, dated 1611,
in the Germanisches Nationalmuseum, Nuremberg.
The painted paper mural depicts musicians playing in a garden
and men and women engaged in amorous dalliance
round a table. Note the painted animals
underneath the benches.

CONTENTS

ACKNOWLEDGEMENTS

WHEN YOU COME, as I do, from a background of writing about full-scale interior design, it would be hard not to be impressed by the style of many of today's miniature interiors, and I have for some time been a true amateur of the art. I love the world of miniatures and I terribly wanted to do this book so that I could have an excuse to see lots of wonderful private doll's houses – which I did.

I could not have even attempted the project without the unquantifiable help of Thalia Sanders, Cotty O'Reilly and everyone else at The Singing Tree doll's house shop in London. They opened their address books, wrote, telephoned and cajoled collectors into letting Nick Nicholson and me see their houses and more importantly photograph them. The Singing Tree also got in special, exclusive pieces for us to show, and designed wonderful room sets for the book, using pieces from their amazing stock. I cannot thank them enough.

I would also like to thank very much the unfailingly kind and helpful press-ganged doll's house owners who showed us much courtesy and looked after us wonderfully. They were Mr and Mrs Marsden-Smedley, Colonel and Mrs Mainwaring, Mr and Mrs Yeldham and Mr Hamish Macdonald. And Miss Lauren Stevens who not only let us photograph her dolls' houses, but was also a source of much infallible information.

Robert Pullin of Hever Castle kindly allowed us to use photographs of John Hodgson's wonderful miniature period settings that are being created for Hever. John Hodgson himself gave much help and encouragement, and Cotty O'Reilly at The Singing Tree and Charlotte Hunt created room sets for us.

I would like to thank both the knowledgeable Nick Nicholson for his patient and expert photography of the miniature rooms, and Derry Moore for his fine photographs of full-sized houses.

Caroline Johnson edited very sensitively, Jane MacAndrew let me change things around without getting cross, and Christopher Fagg kept everything running on a more or less even keel.

It constantly amazes me just how many outstanding miniature makers there are both in Europe and America. Without them there would be no miniature world, and certainly no book.

The lying-in room of the van Amstel house in The Hague. The room is richly furnished, with a 'marble' mantelpiece painted by one of her craftsmen and gilded carving and picture frames. There are four dolls and two babies. The doll on the left of the room is an elegantly attired visitor wearing ear rings and a pearl necklace. The mother is wearing a sort of cloak over a blue dress and there are two nurses, each holding a baby.

PREFACE

ONE OF THE most important points for anyone interested in looking at or creating an interior in miniature, is how each room should actually look. Doll's-house enthusiasts today want to know more than simply which pieces should go in which room. If they are putting together a house in the style of a particular period, or, more usually, in an amalgam of styles, they want to think about why a specific piece of furniture should stand in a particular place, and what colours and patterns should be on the walls and floors. How should the pictures be hung, the bed be dressed, the table be laid? For as in real life, so in miniature: the fascination and beauty of any interior lies in the detail.

Although much has been written on the practical aspects of dolls' houses and miniature rooms, few books have touched on the links between full-scale life and its miniature counterpart — on how things came to be. As well as showing the most beautiful contemporary miniature interiors and craftsmanship available today, *The Doll's House Sourcebook* tries to set the domestic scene for miniaturists and others who are interested in how interiors came to look the way they do, and how people's daily lives affected their living arrangements. After all, every development in the design and furnishing of a house had a reason for coming into being the way it did, whether it was the first eighteenth-century wallpapers designed to imitate the valuable and rare woven wall hangings found in great houses, or the plethora of labour-saving household gadgets produced by the inventive curiousity of the Victorians.

People have always been interested in, and opinionated about, matters of architecture, the arrangement of rooms and interior design, and I have tried to show through contemporary letters and diaries what a few observers of the eighteenth and nineteenth centuries — the period in which so many modern doll's houses are furnished — thought about styles and decoration in their own time, as well as how the patterns of taste and style evolved over the years. My hope is that these voices will charm as well as instruct, and bring even more pleasure to those who, like me, are seduced by the fascinating world of the doll's house.

The shop or storeroom of the Baumler baby house, dating from the last quarter of the seventeenth century, in the Germanisches Nationalmuseum, Nuremberg. On a narrow side table are pots, barrels, boxes, loaves of bread and sugar loaves, all presided over by a diminutive doll.

THE HISTORY OF MINIATURE INTERIORS

Valerie Jackson Douet

IN RECENT YEARS, collecting and furnishing dolls' houses has left the realms of the nursery to become an absorbing pastime for adults. There are many reasons for the almost universal fascination for this world of the miniature, not the least of which is the realistic, three-dimensional picture it affords us of the domestic life of our times. Fashions in interior decorating change so quickly that a doll's house furnished in the style of the 1960s is now as interesting a piece of social history as one furnished in, say, 1900. Thus a collector furnishing a doll's house in the style of today is recording for the future, just as our ancestors were when they created the many fine old doll's houses that still exist in museums and private collections all over the world.

Dolls' houses have not always been intended as children's playthings. Many of the earliest existing models of houses and cooking utensils were funerary offerings, made to serve the needs of the departed when they arrived in the next world. In the British Museum in London, for example, there is a model of a granary, complete with a courtyard in which a woman is grinding barley, which dates from about 1800 BC and other museums have similar models of bakeries, carpenters' and weavers' shops.

Neither was the very first recorded doll's house a toy for a child, even though when Duke Albrecht of Bavaria ordered it to be made in 1557 or 1558, it was ostensibly for his small

The Ann Sharp house, Norfolk, is England's oldest toy house. Ann Sharp was born in 1691, and the house was presented to her by her godmother, Queen Anne.

The dining room in the eighteenth-century baby house at Uppark. Two servants in livery are waiting to serve at table, which is laid with fine glass and silver. There are some fine paintings in this room, some of which may have been painted by Lady Sarah Fetherstonhaugh, others possibly by George Romney.

Throughout the seventeenth and eighteenth centuries, dolls' houses were known as 'baby houses', 'baby' being the name for a doll at that time. From early paintings we know that plenty of humble home-made dolls' houses were made for children to play with, but most of the grander ones still in existence were not intended as toys as we know them. They had a dual purpose; to display the wealth of their owners and to educate the young girls of the family who would later have to run such large houses with their servants and would need to know what to expect.

The earliest known baby houses, which are German, are simple representations of a house, the interiors of which are divided into rooms, with a central staircase. The earliest of all, dated 1611, in the Germanisches Nationalmuseum, Nuremberg, presents a fascinating picture of how life was lived in a wealthy German family in the seventeenth century. The house stands on a wooden base representing the cellar. On the ground floor is a painted Great Hall, where the household servants would have eaten their meals. Apart from the murals (which were copied from an etching by the artist Jan Sadeler), the room is simply furnished with wooden benches, settles, table and chairs. Large pewter plates line the walls above the mural. The floor is painted to look like flagstones, and there is a trapdoor into the cellar. There may have been another dining room for the family on the second floor next to the kitchen, but this was modernized during the eighteenth century and is now a drawing room.

On the top floor is a bedroom containing a huge bed, and a state room with ornate wooden furniture, including a linen press. Women of that time took a great pride in their linen and the daughter of a wealthy family would have been given a good supply of it for her dowry, so presses in German and Dutch dolls' houses are full of bed- and table-linen, as well as of uncut linen ready for making up.

Perhaps the most interesting room of all in this house (and in the other early German baby houses, for there are several) is the kitchen, where there is a dazzling array of pewter plates, as well as jugs, beakers, plates, dishes, ladles, strainers, bowls and platters. At the back of the fireplace is a rack on which the spits used for roasting meat rest, and a 'hastener', a sort of tin container for meat that was placed in front of the fire to speed cooking. The kitchen range with a boiler and oven at the side only came into use after 1780.

daughter. In fact, it was a miniature replica of the house of a German prince, designed to show off his possessions and his lifestyle, and when it was finished the Duke put it in a museum instead of giving it to his daughter.

It was a four-storey building, with a yard, a garden containing a silver well, a stable, a cow barn, and on the ground floor a dairy and other domestic offices. Above were a bathroom, dressing room, kitchen, courtyard, then a ballroom, bedrooms, withdrawing room, a chapel, nurseries and a sewing room, all equipped with silver, tapestries and beautiful furniture – clearly far too grand for a child to play with!

The nursery of the Hammond doll's house, Wallington Hall. Although not a construction of any beauty, the house contains thirty-six rooms filled with a fine collection of furniture. The nursery contains a satisfying assortment of children's toys and a baby hanging from a swing chair suspended from the ceiling.

Even more domestic detail is to be seen in the Stromer baby house, which dates from 1639 and is also in the Germanisches Nationalmuseum, Nuremberg. Here two rooms are furnished as bedrooms. How cosy they must have been with their huge, curtained four-posters and large, business-like ceramic stoves. There are two halls, a reception room and a kitchen even more elaborate than that of the 1611 house. Here, the walls are lined with pewter plates on racks, brass ladles and all the utensils needed to produce a meal. The kitchen also has a board on which household 'wants' were painted (servants were mostly illiterate at that time), graters, a chafing dish for cooking small dishes over charcoal, and a large copper pan with a tap at the bottom to provide hot water. The cooking stove is particularly robust-looking, with a large canopy and metal doors in the base.

The bottom half of the Stromer cabinet is divided into two sets of workrooms placed on either side of the main entrance. These little rooms are furnished in great detail, on one side as a horse and cow byre (complete with carved wooden inhabitants), a wine store containing barrels, a general storeroom and a servant's bedroom, and on the other side as a nursery containing a cradle and baby-walker (a wooden frame that supported a young child learning to walk), a bedroom for the maid, a laundry and a shop with an office.

The shop with an office is a feature of another seventeenth-century German house, a rich merchant's house known as the 'Baumler', also in the Nuremberg museum. It illustrates the seventeenth-century custom of trading from home. Large houses were almost self-contained and here you could buy not only spices and comestibles but also dress materials and other necessities. Here, a large blue cupboard with side shelves contains paper sorted into layers, and on the shelves are sugar loaves, bread, bunches of sponges, weights and scales.

The Bethnal Green Museum of Childhood, London, has an excellent German baby house, dated 1673, which has a working kitchen with weights, moulds, pans and a cooking area under a canopy. A wooden cage on one wall holds an unfortunate bird destined for the pot. There is also a 'state' kitchen next door. Houses of this period often had a 'best' kitchen in which good china and pots were displayed. Two closets are situated at the rear of the state kitchen, a feature seen again in the Dutch baby houses; the back of the kitchen or dining room and beneath the stairs were usual places for conveniences during the seventeenth century.

An English doll's house of about the same period shows how life was lived on a rather less grand scale. The Ann Sharp doll's house is the oldest English example known. It was intended as a child's plaything rather than as a costly toy for an adult, which is one of the reasons for its charm. Ann Sharp was a god-daughter of Queen Anne, who gave her the house some time after her birth in 1691, and the house has been preserved, more or less as Ann left it, by the Bulwer Long family of Norfolk. The complete household is presented to us in wax or wood, all with their names written neatly on slips of paper pinned to their clothes.

The staff required to run a residence even of this modest type was considerable. The baby and the daughter of the house are upstairs with 'Sarah Gill, ye child's maid', 'Fanny Long, ye chambermaid' is in the bedroom, 'Roger ye butler' is standing by the hall table, on the bottom floor we have 'Mrs Hannah, ye house-keeper', in the kitchen is the cook, presiding over a pig roasting on a spit in front of the fire, and in the servants' hall is a footman. All these to serve Lord and Lady Rochett, their son William, 'ye heir', their two daughters and guests.

In both England and Holland, the eighteenth century was the age of the grand cabinet baby house. English baby houses were sometimes based on real houses, with opening fronts and staircases, and some of the smaller ones were actually played with by children. However, the more important ones were big and heavy, status symbols designed by architects to reflect their owners' cultured tastes.

The Nostell Priory baby house is a perfect example of this grand style. Commissioned by Sir Rowland Winn and designed by his architect, James Paine, it was based on the real Nostell Priory in Yorkshire, though it is not an exact copy. The nine rooms have carved panelling and mouldings and contain perfect period furniture, said to have been made by Thomas Chippendale, who as a young man had lived not far away in Otley. It seems probable that this house was an amusement for adults rather than children, who in any case could not have reached the top rooms.

The middle floor of Nostell Priory contains a splendid drawing room decorated with *découpage* scenes on a yellow background. Lady Winn and her sister probably cut out paper prints from books that were especially published about this time for the craft of 'japanning', which was a very popular pastime with ladies of leisure.

An even more elegant English house is the Uppark baby house, which was brought to its new home, Uppark, by Sarah Lethieullier when she went there as the bride of Sir Matthew Fetherstonhaugh in 1747. It has been left untouched and is a perfect time capsule of well-ordered life in a great English country house of about 250 years ago.

The doll inhabitants conform to early eighteenth-century convention in that the servants have wooden heads whilst the gentry have wax heads and are dressed in more elegant clothes. Each lady wears the correct cap and gown and has on the right number of petticoats. The dining room is laid for a meal, with silver table settings under a silver chandelier. Additional lighting is provided by candles in sconces, above which glass shades are suspended to protect the ceiling from smoke. The paintings on the wall are perfect replicas of those found in full-sized great houses, with landscapes in the Italian manner and cattle and sporting scenes. Liveried servants wait to serve the family, who are sitting in the drawing room next door, whilst down in the basement the cook is busy preparing the meal and the housekeeper is sitting in her comfortable room. The four bedrooms are well furnished, each with a four-poster bed, and even the servants' hall has fine oak furniture. Walnut was used for the first floor and ivory for the top floor.

In Holland in the seventeenth and eighteenth centuries, the tradition of fine cabinet houses continued. A beautiful example containing precious works of art and collectors' treasures is the de la Court baby house in Utrecht, but one of the finest is the eighteenth-century Sara Ploos van Amstel house in the Gemeentemuseum, The Hague. Sara's husband was a wealthy merchant and they had no children, so she could well afford the time and money to indulge her passion for baby houses.

The cabinet is furnished on three levels and the rooms are all in boxes, with frames around them to give them unity. Sara purchased it in 1743 to contain her miniatures and rooms, which she had bought at auction the same year. They had previously belonged to the painter David van der Plaes, who had painted the walls of the music room of the house with landscape murals.

Interesting features of the cabinet, reflecting the customs of the time, are a garden room at ground level, placed between the lying-in room and the kitchen, a music room, a porcelain room and an art collection room. The lying-in room, a feature of some Dutch cabinet houses, was presumably also a feature of real-life upper-class houses in an age when married women spent much of their time producing children, not all of whom survived. It is sumptuously decorated with rich hangings and heavy furniture designed to impress visitors, one of whom is seen admiring a baby hidden under a pile of bedclothes in a wicker basket. In some of the Dutch houses the poor babies are completely covered by a cloth, like parrots in a cage, so no doubt this, too, was a custom of the day.

Dutch silversmiths were renowned for their skills and in the music room we find a mirror, fire-irons, a silver wine cooler, a silver foot warmer and a silver cupboard containing silver utensils. There is a great deal more exquisite detail, such as an ivory chessboard, playing cards, dice, smoking materials, a gold inkwell, and musical instruments, including a painted clavichord and a viol de gamba.

The porcelain room was altered by Sara to hold her collection of blue and white 'porcelain', which is actually opaque glass painted to look like the Chinese blue and white porcelain so popular in Dutch houses of the period. Here you can see the shapes that were made for the European market, with the occasional typically Chinese shape given a Dutch handle or spout to please the customer, all displayed on little ornamental shelves, the full-sized versions of which can be seen in the Gemeentemuseum.

The art and curio room at the top of the house is another reflection of the social tastes of the day. Dutch merchants had dealings with cargo ships from all over the world and were able to fill their homes with ivory and amber, spices from the Indies, wines from Madeira and France, glass from Venice and interesting curiosities from far-flung lands. This curio room holds shells, rolls of paper, medals, books and paintings.

Another of Sara's cabinets is to be seen in the Frans Halsmuseum, Haarlem. This house is famous for its silver room and its 'apothecary's study', depicting the astrologer and physician Dr Ludman at work at his desk.

Sara left detailed records of her houses (she had several) in which she wrote down how much everything cost and how much she paid her craftsmen to work on the houses. These uniquely valuable documents are also preserved in the Gemeentemuseum.

In eighteenth-century Germany, there was a breakaway from the cabinet-style house when the Princess Dorothea of Schwartzburg-Arnstadt (1666-1751) devoted her widowhood to the creation of a fully populated dolls' town. Still in existence, *Mon Plaisir*, as the Princess called it, consists of twenty-six houses, eighty-four rooms and 411 dolls, all portraying the life of an eighteenth-century German town as if it were a theatrical event, with dolls acting the parts of royalty, courtiers, servants and citizens.

Daily court life in the princely residence of *Mon Plaisir* shows maids making beds, a royal couple sitting at table, and servants attending their masters and mistresses. In one scene the princess is at her dressing table and in another the prince is being shaved by the court barber. On the table beside him is a largish spoon, which seems an odd item for a barber to use for shaving, but in the days when elderly persons had few teeth, a spoon was placed

Drawing room of the 1903 house at Sandwich. It has a chandelier, a fine, ornate German fireplace, framed portraits, a metal rocking chair and glass-fronted cupboards containing ornaments. A side table is laid for tea and a chess table is set out for a game.

The bedroom of a 1932 Tri-ang house, owned by Valerie Ripley and furnished by Miss Ripley and her sister in the 1930s. It contains most of the familiar brands of dolls' house furniture from that time, as well as home-made items. The house and its contents were packed away in 1939 and remained unseen for forty-one years. You can see some of the ten-piece Tri-ang Queen Anne bedroom suite, which was sold as a boxed set.

commercially made houses were exported by German manufacturers such as Christian Hacker, a Nuremberg toymaker. The finish cannot compare with that of the great craftsman-made eighteenth-century houses, but they have a charm of their own. German and French manufacturers concentrated mainly on doll rooms and shops, possibly because Continentals tended to live in apartments where space was restricted. Because nineteenth-century dolls' houses were intended as children's playthings, those that have survived often contain little bits and pieces of furniture made by their young owners, as well as the German-made miniatures being exported all over the world in huge quantities by enterprising traders towards the end of the century. Soon it was possible to buy everything needed to furnish a mansion. Glass and china, kitchen utensils, upholstery, drapery and plates of food were sold for modest sums, putting them within reach of most children with a little pocket money.

A delightful house that bears this out can be seen at Audley End in Essex. A roughly constructed toy dating from around 1820-40, it illustrates the transition from the fine Georgian baby houses to the mass-produced nursery toys of the later Victorian period. With its brightly coloured wallpapers it was in tune with the fashion at that time for spectacular furnishings, and it is also typical of its era in its mixture of commercial and home-made pieces.

The Audley End house contains some interesting pressed-tin furniture, and also a round occasional table supported on a tripod of simulated antlers, reflecting the German fashion for horn furniture that was created to some extent by the Prince Consort when he bought a set of full-sized horn furniture for Osborne House in 1846. The home-made items show the needlework skills of the original owners. Rooms have full-length silk curtains, the four-poster beds are festooned in matching fabrics, and there are upholstered benches in some of the rooms, as well as bead-embroidered footstools and needlepoint carpets, none of which would have been difficult for the average Victorian Miss to have produced.

Another notable Victorian mansion, containing no fewer than thirty-six rooms, is the Hammond house at Wallington Hall, Northumberland. Again, this is not a remarkable piece of craftsmanship but simply a series of boxes connected by corridors running the length of the house.

Interesting features of this house are the lift at one end and the electric lighting, which must have been an exciting

inside the cheek to fill it out and thus enable the barber to get a close shave! Particularly interesting is the well-equipped palace kitchen, in which the housekeeper and chefs are preparing a meal. There are also market scenes, a card game, a musical gathering, an apothecary's shop, a formal garden, shoppers, shopkeepers, a puppet show, clowns and a fair, all providing insights into the customs of the times. The Princess showed *Mon Plaisir* during her lifetime for the benefit of an orphanage. In spite of wars and political upheaval, her creation has survived and can be seen in the Arnstadt Castle Museum.

By the nineteenth century the craze for baby houses was waning and dolls' houses, which are to some extent a barometer of life in the real world, changed considerably. The Industrial Revolution transformed industry and with the arrival of mass production, dolls' houses became cheaper, enabling more homes to possess one.

Oddly enough, Germany was not a leader of the craft of dolls' house making in the nineteenth century, though some innovation when it was installed in about 1886. Another technical surprise is the fact that originally the water was piped from a tank on the roof to the bathroom and the scullery, a delightful piece of realism that has now vanished due to corrosion of the pipes.

There are rooms of every kind – rooms for servants, for the housekeeper, for children, for storage, a scullery, a drawing room, a governess's bedroom, and a boot room containing an impressive array of bells and a staircase rising to the first floor. The house is filled with a large family of china-faced dolls and, of course, the full complement of domestic staff – maids, nannies, butler, cook, footmen and governess – to look after them.

France, Scandinavia and the USA produced some very fine dolls' houses in the Victorian era, some of which can still be seen in the national museums of those countries. They all mirror the cosy domestic life of the Victorian middle and upper classes with their nurseries, kitchens staffed by cooks and maids, and drawing rooms and dining rooms filled with heavy furniture and dozens of ornaments.

There are few examples of dolls' houses from southern Europe. They come primarily from northern Europe where, because of the climate, life centred on the home. The three great dolls' houses of the twentieth century, Queen Mary's doll's house, Titania's Palace and Coleen Moore's fairytale castle, are in the baby-house tradition, filled with craftsman-made miniatures. But there are, of course, many humbler twentieth-century houses that reflect the lifestyle and architecture of ordinary homes more closely than those extravagant flights of fancy.

After the turn of the century, the toy manufacturing industry in America became well established. Among the most successful leaders was the firm of Rupert Bliss, which made dolls' houses in 'American designs to suit the taste of American children'. Some were exported to Europe, where, if they now appear in auction rooms, they are easily identified by their embellishments of gables, dormers, porches, balconies and turned wooden pillars. They were small and therefore well suited to the small modern home. Some, made of heavy board hinged with cloth, could be folded away, and the firm of Schoenhut made some charming bungalows, featuring turned balustrades on the porches, net curtains at the windows, and lithographed doorways on the walls showing a perspective view of another room beyond.

Most early twentieth-century English houses remained firmly rooted in the past, making few concessions to the shrinking size of the family home. A typical example is a doll's house in the Precinct Toy Collection, Sandwich, which was made by a master carpenter in 1908 when its first owner was three years old. She bought most of the (German) furniture and fittings for it at Hamleys, the famous London toyshop. With its heavy wooden furniture it gives a clear idea of how a house of this period would have looked.

Another typical Edwardian house is in the Bethnal Green Museum of Childhood, London. Called '3 Devonshire Villas', it takes its name from a house in Kilburn, north London, in which Mr Samuel Loebe lived with his family in 1900. Samuel Loebe made it for his daughter, and it is to some extent a replica of the family house, with the furniture too possibly copied from pieces in the real house. The sitting room is quite modern in feeling; the overmantel is painted white, and the stuffed easy chair and sofa are comfortably un-Victorian. Typical of the period are the high picture rail, the standard and sidelights with their silk shades, and a decorative bead curtain covering the door to the conservatory.

By the 1930s, dolls' houses were commonplace. In England, the market was dominated by the Lines Brothers with their Tri-ang houses. In the late 1920s, their 'Stockbroker Tudor' houses became very popular, reflecting a real-life architectural fashion. They were furnished courtesy of 'Tootsie Toy', 'Pit-a-Pat' and others, in a style that many of us can still recall from our childhood. Who could possibly forget the suites of matching furniture, the never-to-be-used fireplaces in bedrooms, the cumbersome wardrobes, or the dressing table blocking the bay window of the semi-detached? In a well-preserved 1930s Tri-ang doll's house such as 'The Gables' (owned by Valerie Ripley) we can see them all again. This house was completely furnished by Miss Ripley and her sister in the 1930s, packed away in a box at the beginning of the Second World War, and unpacked forty-one years later – a nostalgic experience for the sisters.

Now, in spite of, or perhaps because of, the prevalence of plastic in our civilization, there is a renaissance of doll's house artist-craftsmen and -craftswomen who are making perfect miniature reproductions of the houses and furniture of any age you care to mention, keeping alive the best traditions of Mrs van Amstel and the Princess Augusta Dorothea. How pleased those ladies would have been to see such a revival of interest in the world of miniatures.

PERIOD DECORATIVE STYLES

Left: Rebuilt in 1607, Hatfield House is an exuberant example of early Jacobean period architecture in England.
Above: The grand staircase at Hatfield: this is one of the earliest free-standing examples. Above the richly carved balustrade the newel posts bear both figures and heraldic beasts.

I N 1890, the 2nd Lady Monkswell described Lythe Hill Place in Hampshire as ' ... the most perfect place I know. A large and beautiful house crammed with pictures, flowers, *objets d'art*, good servants and people'. As a definition of domestic perfection, it is one with which even now few people would disagree.

The way we look at our home is coloured by the era in which we live. Although through the centuries houses have possessed the same architectural essentials in the way of windows, doors, floors and so on, the manner in which these structural necessities have been embellished, ornamented and made comfortable by successive generations has differed in most, if not all respects. To look at the way in which the dinner plate metamorphosed from a thick slice of bread into a translucent piece of hand-painted porcelain, or how the curtain changed from a practical draught-excluder into a profusion of fabrics and trimmings, is instructive at least, fascinating at best.

Six hundred years ago the house was merely a building that provided basic shelter and warmth for a relatively large group of people. But even though in terms of physical comfort it was primitive, the social structure within was extremely complex. There were as many forms of ritual and rules – spoken and unspoken – as there were later in the so-called 'polite society' of the eighteenth century.

Medieval domestic life centred on the large hall, and with good reason, as it was the only room with heat, the hearth

Berkeley Castle, a twelfth-century fortress in Gloucestershire. This room (above) was originally a chapel. Its timber roof is decorated with medieval ornament.
Left: A deep-windowed room in Berkeley Castle showing its defensive origins.

The Great Hall, *c.*1600, at Longleat House, Wiltshire, continues a medieval tradition.

usually being set in the middle of the room with the smoke escaping through the slatted or louvred roof. Windows were of necessity small. As Witold Rybczynski points out in his fascinating book *Home,* privacy was an unknown concept in medieval society. People ate, played and slept together, with only the sleeping quarters of the master and mistress of the house separated from the rest. With time, however, the concept of privacy grew and the size and importance of the central hall slowly diminished. In country manor houses of the fifteenth century the lord moved from eating on a separate dais in the central hall to dining in a separate room above the hall usually known as the great chamber. By the sixteenth century this space had spawned other, smaller rooms and the idea of separateness evolved.

Progressive as this was, large houses of England and parts of northern Europe were extremely primitive compared to the palaces of the Renaissance being built in Italy, where this was a period of great creative movement and growth, spawning artists of the stature of Tintoretto, Veronese and Raphael, and when arguably as many great works were created on palace walls as on artists' canvases. Houses in the Netherlands and northern parts of Germany were influenced by Italian style and borrowed from its ornamental vocabulary. Italian craftsmen also travelled – in France the palace of Fontainebleau in particular shows many signs of southern influence. But in England, Elizabethan decoration remained simply a richer version of medieval decorative art.

Nevertheless, although the house builders of England may not have been masters of the fine arts, they had already absorbed the idea that architecture, decoration and furnishings were an important part of domestic life. Houses were there to be enjoyed rather than survived. The yeomen classes built small, comfortable manors, farms and town houses, many of which still stand today, whilst the noble and very rich built houses grand enough to receive a king. The typical sixteenth-century English house still centred on a hall, albeit one of diminished size, and contained at least one other large chamber with several smaller rooms. There was sometimes a first-floor gallery, as well as additional servants' rooms. Windows were larger, and there was often stucco ceiling decoration. Walls were partially panelled, usually with oak, and sometimes hung with tapestries or

A typical Italian villa of the Renaissance period. This Classical style spread through northern Europe during the sixteenth and seventeenth centuries.

Hatfield House. The Great Hall, now called the Marble Hall. At the east end is the Minstrels' Gallery.

The ornate carving on doors, screen and panelling owes much to the Italian Renaissance.

painted cloth. Remaining plaster was left plain or painted with simple designs.

By the second half of the sixteenth century Renaissance ideas had spread throughout Europe, aided by the appearance of pattern books mainly produced in the Low Countries. These showed all manner of decorative and architectural styles, including the Classical, and in Germany, Holland, Flanders and England, on panelling and plasterwork, there now appeared national interpretations of Classical grotteschi as well as strapwork and other designs of Italian origin. Southern influence was lessened during the Reformation, however, as links between Protestant countries such as England, Germany and the Netherlands were strengthened.

Architecture and architects were still relatively unknown, but the early years of the seventeenth century saw the emergence of a man whose influence on English domestic architecture was to last for more than a century. Inigo Jones (1573-1652) was conversant, through his travels in Italy, with both extant ancient Roman buildings and also – importantly – with the works of the sixteenth-century architect Andrea Palladio, whose graceful country houses in the Veneto were based not only on Renaissance knowledge but also on the study of ancient Roman architecture and the works of the early Roman architectural writer Vitruvius. The fundamentals of Classical architecture were transported and utilized to great effect by Jones, particularly in his interiors at Wilton and his designs for the Queen's House at Greenwich, built in the 1630s for Henrietta Maria, French wife of Charles I.

At the same time in France the decorative arts reached a glorious peak under Louis X1V, whose reign from 1643 to 1715 heralded the start of France's long-lasting style supremacy. His palace at Versailles, on which work began around 1669, was the natural focus for the work of such designers as Charles Lebrun, le Premier Peintre du Roi, and architects such as Jules Hardouin-Mansart, whose designs were later envied and emulated by the rest of Europe. Jean-Baptiste Colbert, Louis X1V's premier minister, realized the importance of the decorative arts and founded the Manufacture des Gobelins outside Paris, originally to furnish the royal palaces, but it became the centre for all that was best in French decorative art.

The style of decoration associated with the Sun King was hardly subtle. But the sparkling mirrored saloons, the silver and

The State Room (above) of the recently restored Queen's House at Greenwich, London, designed by Inigo Jones (1573-1652). It has a painted and coffered ceiling. The elaborate canopy is in direct contrast to the simple window curtains. The State Bed (left). The hangings are luxurious silver brocade with ornate, richly coloured plumes above the canopy.

gold furniture – all shine, all reflection – were an obvious symbol of the unassailable power of the French throne. It was at Versailles that the salon came into being, and with it the much copied arrangement of rooms 'enfilade', whereby the internal doors of a series of appartments were aligned so that a vista through the rooms was created when the doors were opened. After Versailles this arrangement became standard practice in other European countries, especially in Germany, where many interiors at this time were based on Italian and French schemes, the engravings of court designers Jean Berain and Daniel Marot being particularly influential. Holland, too, had long been influenced by French ideas and decoration. Frederik Hendrik, the Prince of Orange, had a French mother and in the 1630s developed the centre of The Hague in French style.

Things were not quite the same in England, however. Although travellers and ambassadors to England reported back on French and Italian marvels, and Charles II returned from an exile passed in Dutch and French courts with a full complement of Continental craftsmen and artists, once across the Channel French ideas became diluted by Englishness, resulting in a sometimes curious combination of European Baroque – monumental and palatial – with the lighter-toned Classical motifs of Inigo Jones. The result was a unique English Baroque.

This new style is probably best represented by the designs of Christopher Wren (1632–1723). When visiting Paris he had been much impressed by French decoration, including their fine

The Château de Brantes. A Classical French château of the seventeenth century. The central block has the traditional carved pediment, surmounted by a coat of arms and with stone urns set at regular intervals.

Gothick icing-sugar plasterwork at Arbury Hall, Warwickshire. The stucco-work soars, its medieval influences lightened by the taste of the eighteenth century.

plasterwork. Softwood carving, usually in lime, was also introduced by Wren, and is epitomized by the work of the great craftsman Grinling Gibbons (1648–1721), who became instantly famous and admired by all who saw his work. He founded a specialist carving school and its work anticipated the freedom of the Rococo style, with airy foliage, flowers, vegetables and birds apparently suspended in midair.

The Great Fire of London in 1666 accelerated the change in architectural style. The houses that rose from the smouldering timbers were different from their medieval predecessors. Gone were the lowering façades studded with beams, the overslung upper storeys, small windows and dark rooms. The new houses were made from brick and sometimes stone, and were now blessed with good proportions, light and air. They had several separate chambers, different floors were served by staircases that became ever more graceful, and the servants lived apart. Panelling was still in evidence, as were painted designs on walls and ceilings.

Meanwhile, the doughty colonists of America were evolving their own style of living. Furniture brought from Europe provided models for new pieces, and the first frame houses were built and decorated as befitted a young colony. Based on traditional architectural ideas, they consisted at first of a single storey, the overhanging second floor being a later development.

The idea of the house as a base for family and social activity continued to evolve throughout Europe during the seventeenth century. By the end of that century in England and northern Europe a new class, distinct from both nobles and peasants, had emerged of confident, often self-made men who wished to build respectably large, solid houses in which they could live in peace and comfort. In France, too, domestic life, although still formal in content, was changing. No longer did those at court wish to live so much in the public eye, and from the time of Louis XV smaller châteaux and houses were built. These provided far more privacy and comfort, and it was during this period that France began to be thought of as the country from which all ideas of comfort emanated.

Ideas from France stretched as far north as Sweden. Nicodemus Tessin the younger, the Swedish court architect, spent much time there, including three years in Paris during the 1670s, and noted all that was happening, including the marvels of Versailles. Details were sketched and sent back to Sweden,

Japanned chinoiserie by Thomas Chippendale (1718-79) in the state bedroom at Nostell Priory, West Yorkshire.

and after his return north he maintained a close contact with Paris. His own house, Akero, was decorated in French fashion, with the dining room in early Neoclassical style.

During the early eighteenth century sharply contrasting decorative styles emerged in England and France: in France, the Rococo, curvilinear, light designs with scrolls and shell work; in England, rectilinear, Classical solidity after Palladio and Jones. The renewed interest in Palladio's designs was helped by the enthusiasm and knowledge of one man, Richard, 3rd Earl of Burlington, himself an amateur architect, who, on being introduced to Palladio's writings in Italy in 1719, brought the *Fabbriche Antiche Disegnate* to England, publishing it in 1730. The

Rococo did eventually exert its charm in England, but with less resonance than in countries such as Germany and Sweden, manifesting itself in fashions for Gothick and Chinoiserie.

The British gentry were always more at home in the countryside than their European neighbours, for many of whom country estates meant banishment from court. French country houses often reflected little pleasure in pastoral life. More 'urbe' than 'rus', thought Horace Walpole, shade and leaf being eliminated by the fashion of leaving the trees 'stripped up, and cut straight at top'.

In America, the same period saw the emergence of a Classical influence. Symmetry became increasingly important architec-

The Marble Hall at Kedleston (above) designed by Robert Adam (1728-92). Based on a Roman atrium, the niches hold classical statues. An ornate Rococo mirror in the bedroom at Kedleston (right).

turally, particularly in Virginia. Inside the house, wooden panelling was ubiquitous, the materials being easily obtainable. It was usually painted, not in the formal sophisticated tones so liked by the French, but in strong reds, blues and greens.

In the early eighteenth century the architect wielded enormous influence both outside and inside the new house. Alongside his work on the elevation, he not only instructed how each room should look – specifying such details as ceiling decoration, dado and cornice heights and even the design of the door pediments – he also often designed the furniture. This combina-

tion was exemplified by that multi-talented artist William Kent, particularly in the work he did from 1734 with Lord Burlington for Viscount Coke at Holkham Hall in Norfolk.

Thirty years after Kent's amalgam of seventeenth-century Baroque with eighteenth-century Classicism came Robert Adam's own interpretation of the spirit of antiquity. Whereas Kent, and later William Chambers, used Roman temples and palaces as architectural reference, Adam (1728-92) used his own Grand Tour experiences to argue that the ornament of the domestic should be used in decorative schemes. It was this, he felt, that best reflected the art of the ancients. Like the masters of the Renaissance, he also understood the importance of first-rate craftsmen and painters to realize his schemes, as evidenced by his work with Thomas Chippendale (1718-79), who, in *The Gentleman and Cabinet-Maker's Director* (1754), published many of the designs he had created with Adam.

Even had Chippendale not been associated with Robert Adam, the publication of his directory would have ensured his future influence over furniture design. It is no coincidence that the other names known to us today as master cabinet-makers of the eighteenth century – George Hepplewhite (d. 1786) and Thomas Sheraton (1751–1806) – also produced directories of their designs, Hepplewhite's published two years after his death by his widow. Sheraton, in fact, made comparatively few pieces of furniture, preferring to concentrate on his printing ventures, including, between 1791 and 1794, *The Cabinet-Maker and Upholsterer's Drawing Book*. These directories helped spread their influence as far as America, where the designs of Sheraton and Hepplewhite were the inspiration behind the American Federal style, which appeared after the Revolution ended in 1783. This confident style had something in common with French Empire, and indeed with English Regency, but for all that it had a life of its own.

The flame of Neoclassicism flickered for many years. For the next century in Britain – and longer in Europe and America – Classical proportions and ornament continued to be widely employed in both architecture and decoration.

The eighteenth century represents the zenith of the decorative arts. In china, silver, furniture and books, beauty was as important as function. In small houses as well as large, care and attention were given to the business of living in polite society, as opposed to merely living. Detail was everything. Not simply details of pattern and colour, but also of the very structure of domestic life, including comfort and convenience.

The influence of French decoration throughout Europe by this time can hardly be overestimated. The French court had always been the centre to which well-born families gravitated. The architects and designers who conceived the royal grand plan naturally influenced the ideas of those connected with the court, and as a result the houses of even those who had little contact with court life were grander and more formal than their English counterparts.

Neoclassical simplicity at Nostell Priory. The library was designed by Robert Adam with plasterwork by Joseph Rose, and carved and pedimented bookcases by Thomas Chippendale.

In England these new ideas were passed on through the network of neighbouring landowners and their curious guests. As roads and forms of transport became less dangerous and more comfortable, people became more mobile. The London Season for polite society was over by June and the summer was spent on long visits to country houses, with the odd interlude spent taking the waters at fashionable spa towns such as Bath.

By this time there was a new interest in the garden. In Palladio's original houses in the Veneto, and in their later English interpretations, the formal garden had been given no place, the houses in Palladio's Italy being surrounded by working farmland. In England two centuries later, however, it was an altogether more contrived scene. Exponents of the art such as William Kent, Lancelot 'Capability' Brown and, later, Humphrey Repton ensured that lakes were scooped out, hills thrown up and trees uprooted and replanted, all to give the appearance of timeless parkland. Today, Repton's extant red sketchbooks, in which he penned 'before' and 'after' drawings of his patrons' landscapes, are invaluable contemporary records.

The end of the eighteenth century heralded the emergence of what is now called the Regency period – actually from 1811 to 1820. On parallel lines was the French Empire period, both styles stemming from the same roots of linear Classicism, but the French more masculine, even military. Nevertheless, taste of the preceding century still had influence, and an easy elegance was the result.

One of the most innovative and influential English designers and architects of this period was Sir John Soane (1753–1837). A classicist by nature, he understood the ways in which perspective could be employed. His rooms are miracles of sleight of hand, with curved ceilings standing as if unsupported and light apparently coming from an unknown source.

Colour in decoration was by now very important. Until the eighteenth century the majority of houses had been decorated with 'common colours', pale tones that imitated natural materials such as stone and lead. Now, however, the decorative palette became wider and often brighter. Whereas Adam's first schemes were coloured in soft, clear pastels, his later ones were stronger, though not darker. As the century advanced, colours, particularly in textiles, grew brighter still. In decorative terms, it cannot be stressed too strongly how the colours used at the time were far more vivid than they appear to us today. Comparisons with scraps of unused fabric kept in drawers clearly show the devastating effects of 150 years of sunlight on vegetable dyes.

By the beginning of the nineteenth century, although building in the countryside had accelerated, Europe's cities contained the bulk of the population. Richard Rush, American ambassador to the Court of St James from 1817 to 1825, recorded his impressions of London's new houses:

> From the basement to the attics, everything had an air of comfort. The supply of furniture was full. The staircases were of white stone. The windows and beds in servants' rooms had curtains. No floor was without carpeting. In many instances libraries made part of the furniture to be rented with the houses – a beautiful part.

Large cities all over Europe had by now turned into prosperous consumer centres. Goods of all descriptions were made and sold to satisfy the new demand. Paris and London were crowded with shops 'standing side by side, for entire miles'. Silver- and goldsmiths, cut-glass merchants and cabinet makers, all were constantly busy fulfilling the needs of the new middle classes.

But as fast as they strove to meet demands, the new consumer society wanted more. England, for example, though manufacturing much of what it needed, still imported much of its luxury from elsewhere in the world. Richard Rush noted how new houses were crammed with 'porcelain, silk damasks and ormolu from France; marble from Italy; linen from Holland and Saxony; Flanders lace and gems and cashmeres from India'.

Richard Rush's homeland was proceeding along a slightly different decorative path. The story of interior decoration in America during the eighteenth and nineteenth centuries is one of a growing nation – growing in sophistication and confidence, as well as in native craft and industries. By the 1830s America's colonial status was far behind her. Instead the new American culture emphasized self-reliance. Available materials were used: quilts were made from left-over scraps of cloth, walls were decorated with cut-out stencils, and floors were painted or covered with hand-patterned oiled canvas cloth. Eastern cities were naturally more sophisticated than country communities, and New York around 1830 was, as Frances Trollope noted, a city of some style, the brownstone houses comparable to those of Europe:

Victorian clutter at the Linley Sambourne House, London. The perfectly preserved drawing room shows the taste of a prosperous professional illustrator of the 1870s.

The dwelling houses of the higher classes are extremely handsome, and very richly furnished. Silk or satin furniture is as often, or oftener, seen than chintz; the mirrors are as handsome as in London; the cheffoniers, slabs and marble tables as elegant and in addition, they have all the pretty tasteful decoration of French porcelain, and ormolu in much greater abundance, because at a much cheaper rate. Every part of their house is well carpeted, and the exterior finish, such as steps, railings and door frames, are very superior.

In Europe the heavy taste of the nineteenth century was everywhere taking hold. Although decorative cliché has it that almost the entire century was dominated by both excessive and ugly taste, it was in fact only the middle decades that seemed to eschew moderation for monstrosity and elegance for excess. Interestingly, 'elegance' is a word rarely seen in nineteenth-century letters and memoirs. The decline of the word, and the con-cept, was to do – as always – with new wealth and a confident middle class. Like the Tudors, whose architectural and decora-tive excesses are now seen through the soft-edged mists of time, nineteenth-century plutocrats, particularly in England and France, saw nothing wrong in building to impress. Appearance was everything. What was presented to the world was solidity overlaid with a deadening layer of comfort. Layers of cloth and bric-a-brac turned the simple into the elaborate, the slight into the ponderous. For those who had never aspired to such luxuries before, there was an increasing preoccupation with the concept of comfort, although the old landed classes still in some way equated comfort with vulgarity.

The Great Exhibition of 1851 and other, later, exhibitions in both England and France must be regarded as exemplifying both the best and worst of times. On the one hand they represented the extraordinary and innovative industrial advances that had been made. On the other, many of the machine-made exhibits had sunk to new lows of bad taste and inferior workmanship. It just depended from whose viewpoint you looked – that of the

The Great Hall at Abbotsford, in Scotland. Built in the romantic medieval Gothic style by Sir Walter Scott, this was an early example of the later Victorian fascination with the architectural style of the past.

connoisseur who would only accept, and pay for, the best, or that of the new consumer who saw the opportunity to surround him- or herself with the sort of goods previously owned by only the privileged few. Now everyone could furnish their homes in the new taste, and they did with not altogether felicitous results.

This plethora of consumer choice extended into decorative styles, from Gothic and Classical to the hybrid Jacobethan and Scottish Baronial. This last became popular all over Europe, as evidenced by the sudden rash of operas such as *Lucia di Lammermoor*. In England the popular novelist Sir Walter Scott's house, Abbotsford, was a famous combination of olde Scotland and a fairy tale. If these were too strong, there were always others to choose from: Queen Anne or Empire; Indian or Oriental.

The difference between the eighteenth- and nineteenth-century versions of these styles lay in lightness of touch. Gothic style in the 1700s, for example, was exemplified by the wit of Walpole's Strawberry Hill, but the nineteenth century was historically led, with the emphasis on a ponderous accuracy that did little for any artistic aims.

By the mid-nineteenth century, murmurings were heard from groups of men who all shared the belief that interior decoration had reached some sort of crisis point. Some, like Owen Jones, were interested in the academic place and development of pattern and ornament in history. Jones's book *The Grammar of Ornament* (1856) contained more than 100 colour plates of patterns, documenting in fine detail the traditional styles of ancient cultures from Persia to Greece. This work, and his designs for the Egyptian and Alhambra Courts at the Great Exhibition, brought the decorative ornaments of other cultures to a wider audience. The reproduction of ornamental detail was not just a British preoccupation. In France, Racinet published his *Dictionnaire de l'ornement* in 1869, and in Germany there was (I have to check this at office)

Also influential were such artist/designers as William Morris, a man of varied talents who worked in both fine and decorative arts. Although he trained as an architect, Morris's forte was furniture and decoration. He believed it was necessary to remove the artificiality from decoration, advocating a return to essentials in which people had about them only those things they knew to be useful and believed to be beautiful. In 1861 he founded Morris, Marshall, Faulkner & Co, designing 'artistic' papers, fabrics and furniture that reflected the natural life, and working with artists such as the Pre-Raphaelites Burne-Jones and Rossetti. His Arts and Crafts Movement remains influential today.

Other innovative designers whose influence was far more marked than it may have seemed at the time were Edward Godwin and William Burges. Godwin was a little-known decorator whose use of rich colour, dark greens and reds in particular, was so original it still appears startling today, and Burges was a medievalist designer of furniture and interiors whose own house in London was a wonderful confusion of fable, legend and ornament. All these artists waged war on fringed and pelmeted excess.

Carlton Towers. A detail of the decoration of the Venetian drawing room. The moulded plaster walls are gilded to look like leather, and the painted panels show figures from *The Merchant of Venice*.

By the end of the nineteenth century, change was in the air. The cluttered, dense style so loved thirty years earlier was beginning to lose favour, although seen today such rooms would still appear very crowded. Contemporary paintings and photographs show a vast amount of ornamental clutter, displayed without any apparent regard for form or indeed quality. Mantelpieces, sideboards, tables were all submerged under china figures and groups, many of which seem to have been of limited artistic merit.

Slowly, however, there arrived a general lightening of style, which in some homes found expression in a subdued eighteenth-century revival, achieved with new reproductions of

Sheraton's designs and machine-made, papier-mâché 'Adam-style' cornices.

The Aesthetic Movement in England at this time was a self-regarding style, recognizable by its sunflower and peacock motifs and a pallid forerunner to the important design movement that followed it. This was the French Art Nouveau, English Liberty Style and German Jugendstil. As sinuous as the Rococo designs of 150 years earlier, but stronger and more naturalistic, it transformed everything from furniture to light fittings.

But perhaps the most important catalyst of change in the nineteenth century was the arrival of the railways, which from 1840 onwards irrevocably altered the tenor of upper-class domestic

The billiard room at Holker Hall,
Cumbria, with its full-size table, and
large comfortable chairs and sofas.

life, particularly in the country house. Guests would come from Saturday to Monday (never called the weekend) and social life in the country became as important as in the city. Houses became even larger and were altered to encompass new fashions and tastes, as well as boundless leisure. There were drawing, sitting and morning rooms, studies, libraries, smoking and billiard rooms; and for the staff, bedrooms, eating halls and sitting rooms.

A large staff was a necessity, for without a troop of servants no country house could have operated. Organization was essential; the mistress of a large house had to know exactly how to run her small army. Since the seventeenth century manuals had been written both for and by servants and mistresses, and in large houses leaflets were printed giving precise instructions for every member of staff from the second footman to the still-room maid.

Today's nostalgic view portrays the traditional servant as a loyal, healthy, hard-working paragon, but of course it was not always, or indeed often, the case. Many of those who went into service were the impoverished young, drawn to the idea of secure work. The bad pay and long hours were partly compensated for by the lure of regular meals, a bed, clothing and warmth.

In most houses spare time was limited – there was simply so much to do. Not only did the house have to be cleaned daily, but each room, made dirty by the constant burning of coal, had to be regularly and thoroughly turned out and the furnishings lifted, cleaned, repaired or replaced. Water and warmth had to be kept in constant supply, foodstuffs prepared, preserved and stored, and essential household items from candles to cleaning products made – and all this quite apart from any personal whims the members of the resident family might have.

So, not surprisingly, the average servant worked enormously hard, needing strength and physical energy. Hannah Cullwick, a maid of all work in the middle of the nineteenth century, kept a diary, of which this is a typical entry:

> Lighted the fire. Brush'd the grates. Clean'd the hall & steps & flags on my knees. Swept & dusted the rooms. Got breakfast up. Made the beds & emptied the slops. Cleaned and wash'd up & clean'd the plate. Clean'd the stairs & the pantry on my knees. Clean'd the knives and got dinner. Clean'd 3 pairs of boots. Clean'd away after dinner & began the preserving about 1/2 past 3 & kept on till 11, leaving off only to get the supper & have my tea. Left the kitchen dirty & went to bed very tired & dirty.

Many seemingly fixed domestic practices were instigated only because there were servants enough to implement them. For the same reason, many labour-saving inventions and devices failed to gain as much popularity as they might. Domestic plumbing, for example, was slow to catch on because for so long there remained servants to transport the water and waste by hand. Domestic lighting also remained static for centuries. Candles were used for hundreds of years, the most expensive being made of wax. Indeed, the number of candles employed at a rout or assembly was often quoted by guests as evidence of the host's extravagance, or lack of it. Cheaper were tallow candles, but as these were made from the hard yellow-white fat that surrounds animals' kidneys, the smell must have been very unpleasant. Oil was used, often in conjunction with candles, from about 1830 and was accepted by all, but the newly discovered gas lighting was at first deemed by many to be vulgar, and although it was freely available by the late nineteenth century, many houses did not and would not have it. In time, gas became respectable and its vulgar reputation was passed on to the newly discovered commodity of electricity. Domestic electricity was made possible by 1879, and although accepted in principle, its advent was not greeted with unreserved joy, particularly by those ladies who regularly dined in society and whose complexions suddenly became hostage to overbright, barely shaded lamps.

Country houses could also be very cold. Large fires in the principal rooms meant that pockets of often fierce heat were countermanded by the icy blasts found in corridors and passages. When the first central heating was introduced – often a fairly primitive system where water was moved through a series of large pipes along some of the freezing corridors – matters improved, but in many houses this did not come about until the second half of the century.

In both England and America the role of the architect as interior advisor had diminished by the early nineteenth century, but the interior decorator – first seen on the East Coast of America – did not emerge until a hundred years later. The nearest equivalents in the meantime were the large furnishing and decorating companies such as Crace, and upholsterers. As Charlotte Gere observes in her *Nineteenth-Century Decoration*, whilst in the eighteenth century the master of the house and the architect made all decisions about design and decoration, the nineteenth century saw their place taken by the upholsterer. In a far more catch-all guise than we know him today, the upholsterer was the precursor of the twentieth-century interior decorator, advising on colour, paper and furniture as well as on curtains, and, most importantly, working on the whole with the mistress of the house rather than the master. The upholsterer had much influence, and indeed was partly responsible for the excess of upholstery during the nineteenth century. His part of any scheme was always by far the most expensive. The first real interior decorators were American women such as Edith Wharton, better known as a novelist, who wrote *The Decoration of Houses* with

Ogden Codman in 1897, and Elsie de Wolfe, who worked on both sides of the Atlantic and settled in France.

Writing about his early childhood, Osbert Sitwell described the effects of early twentieth-century changes in attitudes towards decoration:

> We settled then, for the first few months of 1900, in 25 Chesham Place … It was done-up in the height of the fashion of the moment, for interior decoration had only just started as a mode and on its present professional basis and Lady Randolph Churchill (the sister of the owner, Mrs Moreton Frewen) had been almost the first person to interest herself in it and may perhaps have had a hand in these colour schemes. Before 1900, the aesthetes alone had shown an interest in the rooms in which they beautifully existed; ordinary rich people had been content to live in the houses in which they lived, with their possessions, ugly or beautiful, about them. They accepted that which fate had decreed, unless a fire, or new circumstances of one kind or another, imposed fresh surroundings upon them. They had not hitherto felt a conscious need for self-dramatisation – but with the turn of the late nineties into 1900, their confidence had all of a sudden wilted. Thus I believe that the rage for interior decoration can be related to the enormous social changes that were only hidden from them by the still shadowy outline of

Change for its own sake has always been a constant theme in the history of interior decoration, as suggested in Mary Carbery's book *Happy World*, where she describes her grandmother 'freshening up' a suite of rooms for her son and his bride in 1861 by' … replacing the Chippendale and Sheraton by heavy mahogany furniture, sentry-box wardrobes, marble-topped washing stands, dressing tables in muslin petticoats, and making Emma's rooms up-to-date with flowered carpets and chintz, in the manner of Victorians and the taste of Hanoverians'. In further chapters we chart some of the gradual, and not so gradual, changes in decoration and furnishings made throughout the house.

THE EXTERIOR

THE ARCHITECTURAL style of a house is as much due to practical considerations, laws, edicts and taxes as it is to the fashions and taste of any one period. In both in the city and the countryside, important houses designed and built by famous architects have always influenced lesser dwellings. Everything from the shape of a window to the design of a door knocker would be noted, digested and often regurgitated in a more practical or economical form, whilst the upwardly mobile often replicated, in miniature, the newest, most impressive great house that they had seen. Partly due to the lack of easy communication between different parts of the country, this process of imitation and reproduction could take many years, thus ensuring the long life of any architectural style.

Early houses were made from the cheapest local materials available. Timber-framed houses usually had an infill of wattle and daub, wattle being thin branches or strips of wood, and daub being mud or clay used as a form of plaster. The timber framing itself was often used to make simple but decorative patterns, and sometime the beams were carved with floral or geometric designs. Timber-framed houses were not necessarily black and white – like so many other conventions of exterior decoration (black iron railings for example), this was a peculiarly Victorian practice. Research has shown that far more colour was used on everything, including statues, and many of these early houses were limewashed and finished in sometimes very bright shades.

A miniature Classical house in the early eighteenth-century period style with the perfect proportions of that time. The double staircase leading to the raised ground floor, the pedimented roof and the external balustrade all proclaim this an example of one of the great periods of architecture.

The medieval house at Hever Castle is a finely detailed miniature example of a late fifteenth-century castle, less fortified than in earlier years and with stone-framed oriel windows set in bays.

In the countryside, roofs, certainly of smaller houses, were almost always thatched, since the materials — usually straw or reeds — were easily available and cheap. Thatching was used for roofing on small rural houses almost continuously until the more prosperous times of the seventeenth century, and then again in the nineteenth century when for reasons of cost it was used on small cottages. In England, tile-making, introduced by the Romans, was once again well established by the fourteenth century, when in parts of the country, houses even at this early stage had clay-tiled roofs. Chimney stacks were found from the fourteenth century on some larger houses, sometimes topped with clay pots. Doorways in larger houses were of stone, the doors themselves made of oak boards, whilst windows were narrow, without glass, and again with a stone surround.

The timber-framed house continued in popularity until the 1500s, by which time the infill, particularly on the bigger houses, consisted of brick as often as it did plaster. If plaster was used, it might well by this time be ornamented with anything from simple scrolls to swirls to painted flora and fauna.

Stone, although plentiful, was not as easy, nor as cheap to work with as wood, and was therefore hardly used at all until the sixteenth century, when improved methods of construction and knowledge of its properties made it, and, to a lesser extent, brick, more popular as building materials. Now, larger houses were often made from the local stone, and even those still constructed of plaster would be built on sturdy stone foundations. Town houses of this period were of timber and plaster or brick, and had two floors with a jettied — or overhanging — top floor that strengthened the structure of the house and maximized the space of the usually narrow plot. The chimneys of Tudor mansions were large, often fantastic and of every shape, generally moulded or decorated with raised patterns, and in marked contrast to the basic stacks on smaller houses. Outer doors were wide, simple, usually made of oak, and hung on iron hinges that could be decorative features in themselves, coming in a variety of shapes and perhaps ornamented. Over the years, windows became larger, although they were rarely glazed except in richer homes. Glass had been available since the 1300s, but was still prohibitively expensive.

In England, unlike in Italy, architects were not much in evidence before the 1600s and during the sixteenth and seventeenth centuries houses therefore grew in an amorphous fashion, each architectural innovation springing from practical needs or developments rather than from purely stylistic considerations. Times were more prosperous, the threat of war less likely and houses reflected this, with larger windows and more care taken over the idea of domestic life.

France and Italy, blossoming in the sun of the Renaissance, architects such as Andrea Palladio (1508-80) who studied the works of Vitruvius and other ancient Roman architectural writers, spread the influence of ancient Rome and Classical architecture, which was soon reflected in the design of houses, including such relatively small decorative details as the external use of capitals, columns and pediments.

By the end of the sixteenth century, some of these influences were to be seen in England, although it was not the pure Classicism of Palladio – that was to come later – but a heavier, Flemish-influenced Classicism that late Elizabethan builders combined with earlier Gothic designs. Larger houses were often E- or H-shaped, with a central porch and sturdy oak door. Symmetrical stone-surrounded windows were made to provide as much light as possible and the rich began to build houses that seemed designed to show off how much glass they could afford. The façade of the famous Hardwick Hall, for example, was described as 'more glass than wall'. The glass itself came in small diamond shapes and was held with lead strips in large bay and oriel windows. These were often many-sided, or even semicircular, and could reach from floor to ceiling. Parts of the windows could open and close, casement style.

The early architecture of America was influenced by the nationality of the various colonists, who included not only the English but also the Dutch, Swedes and French. In the English colonies of the east, wattle and daub was replaced by more weatherproof clapboards – a style that lasted for many years. In England, however, trees had been felled for hundreds of years without thought of replacement, and by the beginning of the seventeenth century there was an acute shortage of timber. Its use was therefore curtailed for house building, and ordinary houses increasingly came to be made in brick or local stone.

Throughout the seventeenth century the Classical influence permeated all architecture and houses everywhere began to show traces of Renaissance Classicism. In England, following the Great Fire of 1666 which destroyed so much of London, fire laws were introduced and new houses were built in brick.

Architects such as Sir Christopher Wren, who continued and expanded the work of Inigo Jones, influenced and consolidated the Classical style in domestic architecture.

Decoratively, the door had become important and was often adorned with a heavy surround or case, that was ornamental in both shape and design. Windows were large, and towards the end of the seventeenth century the sash window was introduced. By the early 1700s, aside from local variations, houses across Europe were well proportioned and based on disciplined rectangular lines, with Classical leitmotifs such as columns and pediments incorporated into the fabric of the building.

In Holland during the seventeenth century, solid, comfortable, red-brick houses were being built with well-proportioned rooms and plenty of windows. The Classical connection was there, but it was less formal and precise than the designs championed by those French, Italian and even some English architects influenced by the work of Andrea Palladio. Dutch links with both England and America were strong at this time and this comfortable style of building could soon be found on both sides of the Atlantic. Popularly called 'Queen Anne', these graceful, well-balanced houses were built for more than a century, underwent a revival spearheaded by Norman Shaw in the late nineteenth century, and indeed are still being built today.

Nevertheless, as far as exteriors were concerned, the most influential architectural movement of the early eighteenth century, in both England and America, was Palladianism. From the 1720s houses were designed with regular façades, the door placed centrally, with an impressive doorcase and often a portico, and the windows in perfect proportion to the whole. The number and position of the windows had by this time became important, for lightness and airiness were now seen as essential. This seemingly simple concept of architecture spread

An archetypically grand house in the Classical style with a massive pedimented central portico mounted on a base of rusticated arches.

Pell Manor, a new doll's house in the Classical style. The owner's initials and the date when the house was built are on a medallion on the pediment. As with so many houses of the period, the Georgian central block has an addition of two wings to complement the main structure.

across Britain and to America, where the influences lasted into the twentieth century.

As the century progressed, the reassuring solidity of Palladian architecture developed into something less pedantic; still Classical, but lighter in tone. These Georgian houses were dignified and always in proportion. Following the Dutch example, more and more windows were sashed and had glazing bars, and in both England and America doors were usually panelled with the traditional four or six panels, depending on the size of the house. The height of a door was a little more than twice its own width. Even the fanlight above the front door was

made into a decorative detail of delight, either divided by wooden bars into relatively simple designs, or shaped into whirls, swirls and curls of cast iron or lead. First-floor balconies were made from iron, often using formal, Classical motifs in the design. Large houses were constructed in Portland stone, smaller ones in grey or red brick. Many houses were finished in stucco plaster over brickwork; sometimes the stucco covered the whole building, sometimes only the lower storey. Originally it was left in its natural stone colour, but later came to be painted in various light-toned shades. Roofs were generally tiled with grey Welsh slate, but chimneypots were available in several hundred different designs.

One other eighteenth-century architectural movement that influenced the exterior far longer than it did interiors was Gothick. Based on the passion for romantic medievalism, it was popularized by Horace Walpole, who began to restyle his house in romantic medieval fashion in the 1750s. This amalgam of early Gothic with the Classical and a dash of legend and fable resulted in houses being built with castellated projections, arched windows and doors, and curving window bars. Such features became very popular, and were incorporated or added to existing houses for the next hundred years.

During the late eighteenth century the terrace came into being as an elegant solution for those members of Georgian polite society who cared to spend some time in town. Here again Palladian principles were employed, although in a more elongated version than that used in villas. The lines of these terraces were rectangular and linear, but graceful rather than hard. Architecturally, their beauty was enhanced by Classical columns and pilasters used along the full height of the building. The tall and elegant sash windows on the *piano nobile* – the principal (usually the first) floor – of these houses were complemented by iron balconies, the designs of which were freer in style, with naturalistic leaves and flowers winding their way along the ironwork. John Nash, architect to the Prince Regent and responsible for the elegant terraces of London's Regent's Park, refined the form and influenced terrace building for many years. The popularity of the terrace was much more marked in England and Holland, as well as the new cities of America, than it was in the rest of Europe. Italian and French cities tended to have houses that looked in, not out, and were often built around central courtyards.

As time progressed, both terraced town houses and the new low-built villas continued to be finished in stucco but now often sported elegant curved verandah roofs in iron over the balconies, as well as cast-iron porches. In France, houses remained faithful to the Classical mode in both the cities and in the countryside.

In America, houses during the Federal period (1789 to *c*.1830) were built in traditional Georgian in style, touched with a local Palladianism, but towards the end of the eighteenth century a new, more academic form of Neoclassicism evolved, known now as Greek Revival architecture. This drew heavily on Classical references, and although used primarily on public buildings, Classical decorative motifs were used extensively on houses in both the South and East up to the middle of the nineteenth century. Although some grander houses were finished with stucco, many were still finished with wooden boards. When combined with Classical pediments, columns and porticoes, not to mention, in the South, the essential shady verandahs, this presented a style that was wholly New World.

In England, early Victorian architecture courted an amalgam of styles both in the town and country. Terraces were built in even greater numbers, but the lines became clumsier and the elegant sweep of earlier schemes was missing. These terraced houses tended to be taller and narrower than their predecesors in order to maximise the available space in fast-growing cities. The façades were not as flat as they had been, and many houses sported a squared-off bay on the ground floor. Front doors were squarer in shape, with any glass panels above the door tending towards the rectangular. Plate glass in sheets was fairly widely available from about the middle of the century, and as a consequence windows became larger and wider.

At the same time, villas and semi-detached houses embraced a variety of decorative forms, from a sort of Italianate, as opposed to Classical, ornament, to the full-blown pastiches of the Jacobethan and Gothic styles. The latter became extremely popular architecturally and was used in town as well as in country houses, with faux-medieval ecclesiastical decoration embellishing both windows and doors.

In Europe, the end of the century saw the Arts and Crafts Movement and Art Nouveau take some hold on the interiors of houses, but on the whole neither style greatly influenced external architecture – with some notable individual exceptions such as Leighton House in London. The façades of late nineteenth-century houses were not unappealing, however. Many of them had large windows, and these could be ornamented with different panels of glass, often coloured. Glass was treated almost as an artist's canvas and painted with anything from geometric designs to pastoral landscapes and stylized portraits. The new wide front doors – often surrounded with specially designed decorative tiles – had both central and side panels of glass that were ripe for decoration.

The dawn of the twentieth century saw a new nostalgia for many of the architectural styles of the past, from half-timbered and whitewashed villas to narrow Georgian-style terraces, creating at times a kind of architectural free-for-all. During the 1920s and 1930s, one new style called Art Deco in England and International Modern elsewhere – made the attempt to streamline architecture and rid it of functionless ornament. Although relatively short-lived, the movement had an influence on the general simplification of line both within and without the house that remains with us today.

A detail of one of the rounded windows on the *piano nobile*. The balustrade design encompasses gilded crowns amongst the finely wrought ironwork.

The Palace of Versailles in miniature, by Kevin Mulvany and Susan Rogers. This section shows the imposing central block of Louis XIV's palace, surmounted by a clock held up by stone figures.

A further detail from Versailles: an *oeil de boeuf* window set into the hipped roof. The stone surround features a mask, leaves and swags.

John Hodgson's Georgian House at Hever Castle, a severely Palladian mansion faced in stone blocks, rusticated to the *piano nobile*.

THE EXTERIOR

This miniature exterior represents a late seventeenth-, early eighteenth-century house of red brick and stone with a hipped roof and a central block, the pediment of which is curved in the Dutch manner.

Bernard Hall by Paul Wood. This
Palladian mansion is the epitome of
grandeur – right down to the last
clopped bay and window box.

A fine miniature house in Queen Anne style. Long and low-built in red brick, simple in its proportions, and with little decoration, this recognizably late seventeenth-century English house owes something to the architecture of the Netherlands.

A Palladian doorway with
surrounding stone blocks set in a fan
design that echoes the fanlight above
the door. Both the shallow steps and
the door are framed by elegant
wrought-iron railings.

With its stuccoed finish, central
door delineated by double pilasters
and pediment, and boldly framed
windows, this miniature represents
the type of unpretentious eighteenth-
century English house found in
many a market and county town.

A splendidly detailed Regency house. The low-pitched roof, golden-coloured brick, curved ornamental fanlight, and iron canopy over the elegant first-floor balcony all proclaim this to be influenced by architects of the late eighteenth or early nineteenth century.

A typically narrow, but still elegant, town house – one of an early nineteenth-century terrace. The ground floor windows are shuttered and each window on the first floor has its own set of simple railings, although the railings at street level are more ornate.

In miniature, a late example of the eighteenth-century Gothick style that was so popular from about 1750 onwards. The gables of this stuccoed house evoke church architecture and the front door that is also reminiscent of medieval buildings.

A fine representation of a nineteenth-century grocer's shop with living accommodation above.

An early branch of Marks & Spencer, then a penny bazaar, now a worldwide chain. The style is typically late nineteenth century, with wide plate glass windows, a curved arch over the entrance, and a rather monumental pediment whose decorative elements bring to mind the lines of Art Nouveau.

An English country cottage. This two-storeyed dwelling is typical of lath and plaster cottages which are still found all across the English countryside.

A typical 1930s house from the London suburbs. The so-called 'Stockbroker Tudor' style was built in great quantities but not all examples were double fronted and had garages.

THE HALL

A detail of the hall of Kevin Mulvany's miniature Versailles, where intricate paintwork has resulted in immensely grand decoration in the Renaissance manner. From the elaborate Ionic columns where plinth, base and shaft are all of different marbles to the gilding used to outline mouldings and cornice, this is a room intended to impress and intimidate.

THE WORD HALL is all that we have left to remind us of the time when the Great Hall was the heart of the house, the central meeting and living place for the whole family. In medieval times it was simply one large room – usually the only one with a fire – and the entire household took all meals there. Gradually it evolved into a more elaborate room and by the sixteenth century was often two storeys high with a fireplace in one wall and windows on both sides. There were carved wooden partitions or screens at one end and a platform dais at the other. Beyond the screens lay the kitchen and often the buttery. By this time the lord of the manor had retired to new, smaller and more private rooms where he and his family ate, and the hall was used only for formal banquets. The rest of the time it was the domain of the remaining household and servants.

Furniture in this room was sparse, and at the beginning of the seventeenth century might consist of one or more long tables, benches lining the walls, and cupboards or buffets. The walls might be hung with arms, flags or banners interspersed with the heads of animals killed in the hunt – a style of decoration that was to re-emerge two hundred years later in less rugged surroundings.

By the middle of the century the Great Hall was beginning to shrink in size and had taken on the more specific function of the area within the house where servants and visitors waited to be seen. The hall at Coleshill House in Berkshire for example (designed by Roger Pratt in the 1640s, but now destroyed), had,

The hall as gracious ante-room, furnished in eighteenth-century splendour. Tall blackamoors frame the formal display of table, rug and sculptural dried flower arrangements standing in the arched niches.

said Celia Fiennes in 1687, 'a hall paved with black and white marble and seats round the room cut in arches in the walls.' Those other activities that had once taken place in the hall now had specific rooms of their own.

A century later, halls in both town and country houses had developed into very different rooms. In most town houses, other than the very grand, the hall had diminished in size, and was used simply for the reception of servants, visitors of rank waiting in the appropriate ante-room, of which there were sometimes several. The narrowness of the elegant new Georgian terrace houses meant that the hall, too, was narrow, often no more than a corridor lit by a fanlight above the door. In larger town houses, however, as well as in the country, the hall remained large and was used not only as an antechamber but also as a dining room and a place for parties and recreation generally. Rising to the height of the house it was much more a reception room than a waiting room and contained the central staircase, which was often an imposing feature in its own right, perhaps circular in design and constructed from the finest materials.

Decoratively, the hall was often looked on as a sort of opening statement for the rest of the house, particularly in larger properties, such as Holkham Hall and Kedleston Hall – the former the work of William Kent, the latter of Robert Adam. Both are very dramatic, promising much of the rooms beyond. At Holkham the hall, known as the Marble Hall, rises almost the full height of the house with a domed and coffered ceiling supported by Ionic columns in Derbyshire alabaster. The hall at Kedleston, also named the Marble Hall, was modelled on a Roman atrium with twenty huge columns of Nottinghamshire alabaster and niches in the walls holding statues of Roman gods and goddesses. In many houses like these the hall was as significant as the state bedroom in speaking of the power and standing of the owner. Along with the other important reception rooms it took up the central part of the house, leaving kitchens, small rooms and even bedrooms in less convenient areas.

As the other reception rooms of the house increased in importance, the hall became proportionately less necessary, becoming on the whole by the early nineteenth century an area where comings and goings took place and were recorded. With the popularity of the terrace, the hall became ever more narrow, until it was often no more than a corridor.

During the middle years of the nineteenth century, however, there was a move to reinstate the medieval glory of the hall, and this coincided with the popularity of the nostalgic baronial and Gothic styles. Although relatively few new Great Halls were constructed – those that were, were usually in the rambling new–old houses being built by the rich – there was a popular decorative fashion for hanging on the walls in the manner of eighteenth-century trophies such military and sporting paraphernalia as guns, swords and armour, as well as more basic sporting reminders such as the heads of stags. Remnants of this trophy style can still be seen today.

Those Victorians who did not embrace the baronial–industrial style – that is to say, the majority – furnished the corridor hall in exactly the same way as they did the rest of the house. Lighting was dim, walls were covered with multipatterned or embossed paper, and woodwork was stained dark. Furniture would include tables, chairs, a hall stand, possibly a wooden settle, and at least one palm in its pot, this last form of adornment considered essential by a large part of the middle-class population.

The Victorian enthusiasm for gadgets and inventions, including the uses to which the new electricity could be put, was also apparent in the hall. At the end of the nineteenth century, the Manners family moved into a house in Arlington Street in Mayfair, originally decorated by William Kent in 1741. Diana Cooper, the Manners' daughter, described how the eighteenth-century surroundings had had various Victorian enthusiasms superimposed on them:

> When the front door opened [visitors] found themselves in a darkish pillared hall, to the right of which was a wide and shallow stepped staircase of stone, beautifully balustraded in wrought iron …The narrow back stairs went up five stone flights with an iron banister curved outwards to give place to ladies' hooped skirts – a pre-crinoline line. Between these banisters there just fitted a labour-saving letter box slung between two leather straps and worked by a top-floor wheel and a basement handle. The procedure was to communicate from the top floors by an echo-age telephone, saying to the cave-dweller, 'I've put some letters in the box,' and he would rush to manipulate the handle. Another device was a small electric gadget on the

The Great Hall of the Medieval House at Hever Castle. This was the communal room for the family and its household, furnished with long tables, benches and cupboards for displaying the plate, and lit by the new-style large windows suggestive of church architecture. There is an open fire in the centre of the room.

An imposing eighteenth-century hall with a double staircase that curves round to meet on a half landing. The floor of black and white marble diamonds contrasts with the white stone of the stairs and balustrading.

wall by the front door which, when a little lever was pulled down, would produce in a short time a child of nine dressed in heavy blue serge uniform, a pillbox hiding one ear, who would for sixpence encircle any distance in forty minutes, bearing letters or parcels.

Towards the end of the century, together with the rest of the house, the decorative appearance of the hall became less heavy. There was less furniture on view, and this had the immediate effect of making the space seem larger and lighter, though artificial lighting itself was better, giving a welcoming rather than an oppressive effect. The hall was again beginning to be seen as an important part of the impression a house might make on a guest, and many newly built houses had larger, often squarer halls, with a turned staircase.

An integral part of the hall since medieval times has been the staircase, which has gone through various manifestations of grandeur through the centuries. Thirteenth- and fourteenth-century houses often had no stairs at all, a ladder or an outside set of steps giving access to the upper floors. During the Renaissance in Italy and France, however, sumptuous and monumental staircases were built, usually in stone. The staircases in England at this time were of wood and simple in construction, although as the century progressed they became broader and more decorative. By the 1600s, large houses had great staircases built in timber, and throughout the seventeenth century the central stairs sported a riot of carving and decoration on balusters and handrails and particularly on newel posts which were carved into complex shapes. In Germany at this time the hall and the vestibules or landings above were often used as adjuncts to the living areas, in particular as places to house the huge carved and corniced cupboards that were then so popular.

In grand houses in England and Europe marble had become a suitable material for staircases by the seventeenth century. Balustrades were often of iron, and the staircase itself became bigger, gradually occupying a more prominent position. Few, however, were as fine as the Duke of Chandos's staircase in his house Cannons in Edgware, which, before it was demolished in the early nineteenth century, was made of blocks of Italian marble twenty feet long, with handrailing wrought in silver.

The idea of the magnificent staircase was fully developed in England and America by the early eighteenth century. In grand houses soaring steps were of marble or stone, often in two branching flights that reunited on a higher landing, the stairs complemented by ornamental balustrades. Both walls and ceiling could be decorated with brio: scenes of antiquity, pastoral landscapes, or angry skies. In more modest houses too, the staircase became a thing of elegance and beauty. Gently curved handrails framed fine balusters, these last often turned into intricate carved designs. The barley sugar twisted rail became popular in America, and often even the sides of the stairs were decorated with a fluted curve.

During the eighteenth century the hall and main staircase also became a place to hang paintings, though usually not the most valuable, and in the country often those associated with sporting activities or country pursuits. More often, the hall became a showplace for sculpture, particularly those acquisitions of the antique variety brought back from Grand Tour travels in Italy. Niches were set into the walls to hold such pieces.

The fashion for complex stair decoration more or less disappeared at the end of the eighteenth century. For most of the nineteenth century, staircases in smaller houses had plainer rails and posts, with a handrail that was curved, smooth, and usually made of mahogany, although the newel post still retained some of its earlier decoration, a necessary decorative feature in the new, narrower hallways. Towards the end of the nineteenth century, however, the new factories with their ability to mass-produce cast iron meant that many late nineteenth-century houses, in England, France and America now had iron balusters that were no longer simple sticks; instead, intricate ovals, cartouches and medallions ran beneath the handrail, though the latter was usually still made of wood.

The hall floor was always of decorative importance. During the seventeenth and eighteenth centuries, floors in the halls of larger houses were often tiled with a local or Portland stone, the

A rich and stately reception hall in the miniature Versailles, one of an enfilade of rooms. Behind the balustrading is a handsome lacquered chest, the colours of which are echoed in the gilded stools in front of the balustrade. The parquet floor is laid in an elbaborate chequered design.

A simple hall in an eighteenth-century country house. There is real elegance in the gently curving staircase, the airy iron balustrade and the Portland stone floor. The collection of Classical stone ornaments serves as a foil to the simplicity of the setting.

The next chamber in the sequence of rooms at Versailles, this ante-room is of suitably majestic appearance. The domed ceiling above the marbled and gilded walls is painted with scenes depicting the triumph of the king. A gilded trophy and coat of arms are set into the ceiling.

squares sometimes intersected with smaller squares of black marble. Black and white marble arranged in geometric patterns was the other traditional option. At first used only in larger houses, by the nineteenth century it could be found in houses of all sizes. By the end of the century, ceramic and stone tiles were used almost as mosaics, with all sorts of intricate and coloured designs being created.

The Victorians were also very keen on what they called parquet, originally known as parquetage. A floor treatment used in both France and England in the seventeenth century, it originally consisted of intricate patterns of different coloured woods. By the nineteenth century, however, the procedure had degenerated into a simple pattern of woodblocks, which were often laid in a herringbone design. During the 1860s, the narrow hall floors of smaller English houses were covered with an early type of patterned linoleum, sometimes called a floor cloth, which was the either width of the passage, or was bordered with a strip of coloured paint matching the pattern.

In America, because much of the East Coast was extensively forested, the most obvious floor material was wood. In 1871, the English naturalist Marianne North, was travelling there, and in Quincy, Massachussetts, visited the descendants of the early American presidents John Adams and John Quincy Adams. The house, one of the oldest in America, made much use of wood:

> The floors, staircases and chimneypieces were of different sorts of wood – black walnut, butternut, hickory, ash and pine – beautifully put together, with very little ornament, sometimes a line or simple geometric pattern cut and filled with blue or red, and the rich natural colour of the wood kept as a groundwork....there was one room wainscotted with polished mahogany.

Sometimes less fine wooden floors were painted, and these simple painted floors developed into stencilled patterns, a technique now indelibly associated with early American art.

It is interesting that, in our own century, narrow corridor halls are, in many houses, incorporated into the ground floor rooms, either by design or alteration. Perhaps this could be seen as a modern return to the way of life enjoyed in the medieval Great Hall.

There is Classical grandeur in the
double-height hall of the Georgian
House at Hever Castle, where the
imposing staircase and gilded
balustrading dominate the scene.
Marble columns rise from a marble
floor, the black and white pattern of
which was very popular during the
eighteenth century. On the walls are
Reynolds's *Lady Eglington* and two of
Stubbs's equine paintings.

THE HALL

A hall that shows how the architecture of a large house can be applied to smaller homes and yet remain in perfect proportion to the whole. In this town house the staircase that dividing at the first landing into two flights is as elegant as its grander inspirations. Note also the Classical circular inlay at the base of the stairs.

A sophisticated hall belonging to a town house. The simple lines and decoration of the floor and staircase are brought into relief by the dramatic columns, the base and shaft of which are in contrasting marbles. The classic wooden staircase has white painted sticks and a turned mahogany handrail.

A small country hall used as much as an extra sitting room as a thoroughfare. A feeling of comfort is created by the flatback figures on the mantelpiece, the domed flowers, the brass-potted plants and, especially, the miniature basket of knitting.

A country hall ready for weekend pursuits. The suitcase to be unpacked, the diminutive riding boots that wait for a rider, the umbrella in the stand, and the mounted stag's head all suggest the outdoor life.

A nineteenth-century town-house hall filled with grandfather clock, ceramic stick and umbrella holder, petit-point rugs, two tables, and the essential tiny top hat.

A hall designed and furnished in the elegantly rectangular style of Charles Rennie Mackintosh, the turn-of-the-century Scottish architect. All the pieces are miniature replicas of his designs.

THE DRAWING ROOM

ALTHOUGH the traditional drawing room is no longer essential, until recently most large houses had at least one formal room. The medieval English house had the one communal room, but by the sixteenth century, many English houses contained a solar or withdrawing room in addition to the first-floor great chamber, and often a smaller, warmer parlour on the ground floor. In France and the Low Countries, there were also warm, tapestry-hung parlours where the family sat.

During the sixteenth and seventeenth centuries, life in England, as well as in Italy, France and the Low Countries, was still very much divided into formal and informal living. During the seventeenth century in Europe, the formal room became known as the salon, or saloon, and was part of a group of state rooms. Around it grew up other rooms in which family life could continue on an informal level.

The Italian decorative influence was strong. In France it was taken on wholesale, although in Germany and the Netherlands it was softened by wall-hung textiles. Britain took its style from the Germans and the Dutch, particularly after the Reformation, when Europe's Protestant countries formed closer ties.

Seventeenth-century living rooms were often panelled, the small rectangular oak panels of the sixteenth century giving way to larger, simple ones of pine painted green, blue or brown, or sometimes marbleized in black-veined white.

At the beginning of the seventeenth century windows rarely

A sophisticated drawing room furnished with pieces from the eighteenth and nineteenth centuries. The gilded legs of the matching pier tables are picked up in the *trompe-l'oeil* balustrading. The elegance of the blue silk chaise longue is emphasized by the extraordinarily elaborate flower arrangements.

81

had curtains, and those that existed were more utilitarian than decorative. Gradually, though, windows became more important decoratively. In England curtains were hung in pairs on rings and poles, whilst the more sophisticated French and Dutch often used fabric *en suite*, with chairs, windows and bed hangings to match. Floors were covered with rush mats, particularly in colder countries such as Flanders and northern Germany, for although carpets were now available, they were valuable possessions and usually displayed draped over tables.

Lighting was poor, one of the reasons why the chimneypiece remained the focus of a room, giving both heat and light. In France and England glass chandeliers were only to be seen in the richest of houses, but in the Netherlands a brass version was widely used.

In decorative terms, the early part of the eighteenth century was dominated by the concept of formality. The first Palladian houses, whilst Classical and simple outside, were elaborate inside, with strong colours and surface decoration. In large houses walls might be painted with romantic, ruined landscapes, whilst in smaller houses white walls contrasted with dark brown woodwork. Later in the century such Palladian architecture and decoration was adopted by the Americans, encouraged by the erudite enthusiasms of such men as Thomas Jefferson.

At the same time as Palladian-inspired Neoclassicism was being preached in England, another decorative wave rippled in from France and then Germany. It was the Rococo, and from about 1720, rooms were being designed in this new sensuous, sinuous style. In France the shape of the Rococo room remained basically rectangular, but in Germany, where the style was adopted enthusiastically, the room became as fluid as the decoration, with stucco work that seemed to defy architectural confines.

In England the Rococo was not wholeheartedly embraced, but elements of it were used in other styles, including Gothick, which combined authentic Rococo with self-parody and wit. The style became quite popular, and many was the drawing room that sported arched windows, fretwork screens and medieval ornament. Then there was Chinoiserie, popular in Germany as well as in England, where it was still being used nearly a century later by the Prince Regent in his Brighton Pavilion. Chinese motifs, finely moulded in stucco and painted, appeared on walls and ceilings, sometimes following such academic examples as William Chambers' 1757 *Designs of Chinese Buildings*, but more often inspired by any vaguely oriental motif.

In 1758 Robert Adam returned to England from Italy, where he had been with his brother James and mentor Charles-Louis Clérisseau, the French architect and writer. It would be no exaggeration to say that from that time the face of English interior decoration was changed for ever. Robert Adam was important to the development of the English interior on many levels. He gave interior decoration a domestic, attainable scale, and brought to it a new warmth and life. Although he was an exponent of the Classical rather than the Rococo, he understood the latter and his Classical interpretations, using the ornaments of ancient Rome and Greece, created rooms to which his contemporaries responded enthusiastically.

He also made much use of stucco, employing it not only on the walls, tracing the lines of the once ubiquitous, now unfashionable, panelling but also using it on ceilings in elaborate designs. This did not go unnoticed on the other side of the Atlantic. The stucco decoration on the hall ceiling in Thomas Jefferson's Neoclassical masterpiece Monticello, for example, is a fine example of the growing sophistication of American interiors.

Eighteenth-century English walls were usually painted or papered, although fabric was still often used in France, particularly the fresh designs of toile and chintz. Paint colour was, to a degree, determined by income. Simple wood tones like walnut and cedar were cheaper than stronger tones such as gold, olive, Prussian blue, orange and pink. Most expensive — and therefore impressive — was a deep green that cost several times more than the basic shades. In America panelling was still popular, on chimney walls in the North, covering the entire room and often painted in the South. Wallpapers, frequently block-printed, were used where panelling was not.

Although wallpapers have been found dating back to the early sixteenth century, they were not manufactured in any quantity until the last decades of the seventeenth century. The hand-painted Chinese papers imported by the East India Company were copied by both the English and the French. Designs, in panels, were continuous and often depicted a pastoral or legendary scene. English wallpapers, particularly flock — made by sticking powdered wool to paper — were fashionable in France, and known as '*papiers d'Angleterre*'. A potted social history can be seen in extant wallpaper fragments, for the

A Swedish drawing room of the eighteenth century decorated in the light colours typical of that time – white, grey, blue, pale yellow and gold. The lightly Neoclassical painted wall panels are also characteristic of Scandinavian decoration of this period. Central to the room is the essential faience tiled

enthusiasms of the day were often transcribed on to paper. Greek and Roman motifs were popular during the Grand Tour decades, as were Eastern – particularly Turkish – designs in France. Later, Napoleon's successful military campaigns also became suitable wallpaper subjects.

It remained unusual for carpets to be used as floor coverings in the drawing room, other than in the most palatial of settings. All across Europe they were still displayed on tables and covered when the table was needed for a meal. Although there were cheap carpets and mats ranging from rushes to linen or oil-cloths, it was not obligatory to cover the floor. Bare boards sufficed, not shining with the high gloss of today, but glowing with the dull sheen that comes from being dry-scrubbed with sand. After 1750 English companies like those at Wilton, Axminster and Kidderminster began to make carpets, usually at this stage reserved for the principal rooms. Grander French houses often had floors laid with an elaborate design of wooden parquetry or inlay, whilst in America floors and floor cloths

A second view of the Swedish drawing room (previous page) the tile stove is picked up in the painted wall panels. The sofa is treated more as a day bed, with curtains that hang from a central dome.

were painted or stencilled. During the first half of the eighteenth century this developed into an art form, often imitating the woven carpets that were not as yet easily available, although by about 1760 both European and Eastern woven carpets could be found in more prosperous American homes.

Windows became increasingly important throughout the eighteenth century. The festoon curtain was introduced to England from France, which by the end of the century, was designing ever more fantastic curtain ideas that incorporated a veritable symphony of swags, drapes, tassels and pelmets.

In America, textiles had originally been spun at home, but from the early 1700s these simple weaves were augmented by fabrics imported from Europe. Damasks and velvets were popular and widely used, but by 1782 John Hewson, an English calico printer, had set up his own manufactories and attention again turned to home-produced textiles. In Europe, high-quality block-printed chintzes had been available to those who could afford them for some years, but the patenting of Arkwright's spinning frame (1769) and Cartwright's power loom (1785) brought cheaper printed chintz within the reach of most.

Important changes occurred in the shape of drawing-room furniture over the course of the eighteenth century. Not only did

tables, chairs and other pieces become lighter – as seen in the designs of Messrs Chippendale, Sheraton and Hepplewhite – but during this period the French introduced the idea of upholstered furniture, an important step that brought new elements of comfort and informality to Europe. Straight-backed chairs were still used, but together with deep, well-upholstered armchairs with winged or curved backs. Also introduced were day beds and sofas with closed ends.

As the pattern and design books of the great English cabinet-makers travelled swiftly across the Atlantic, American sitting-room furniture became more sophisticated. The so-called English Rococo, as described by Thomas Chippendale in his 1754 work *The Gentleman and Cabinet-Maker's Director*, was interpreted with a new simplicity by new master cabinet-makers of the East such as Thomas Affleck. Upholstered furniture arrived here too, particularly in the form of high wing chairs and well-padded sofas.

By the late eighteenth century the drawing room or saloon remained formal whilst other, smaller rooms provided intimacy. Entertainment was varied. In both England and France there was a craze for card games, and contemporary diarists complained that conversation and reading had become redundant. Every fashionable drawing room had enough small tables for brag, quadrille, whist, and loo. Other tables were needed for reading, writing and drawing, as well as for sewing, and for the making and taking of tea. Tea, coffee and chocolate had been fashionable ever since first imported by the East India Company. Drawing-room tea caddies to store the precious leaves were prized possessions. Made from fine woods, they were decorated with inlay or marquetry, and always fitted with a strong lock.

Silversmiths in both England and America produced elegant long-necked coffee- and chocolate-pots, along with small, pear-shaped teapots that needed refilling from a kettle kept warm on a burner and stand.

Guests sat on light, elegant chairs carved with Prince of Wales feathers, anthemion, shields or hearts. There might be settees – often part of a group with the chairs – sofas for reclining and small stools. Pier tables stood between windows, side tables, hinged Pembroke tables and unhinged sofa tables stood elsewhere. The chimneypiece no longer dominated the room. The elegant fireplace housed tongs, shovels and pokers and was fronted by a pair of chimney boards painted with birds or flowers. In the rest of Europe, particularly in Germany and Scandinavia, stoves were still used, and could be very ornate, sometimes made of glazed earthenware or cast iron.

This plethora of equipment meant that the room layout had to change. Where chairs had been kept against the walls and then drawn into the centre to form a conversation circle, the new furniture now began to fill the room. This coincided with a desire to change the old-fashioned circle. Fanny Burney writing in 1779 described the drawing room of the famous bluestocking, Mrs Vesey:

> Mrs Vesey's … fear of ceremony is really troublesome; for her eagerness to break a circle is such, that she insists upon everybody's sitting with their backs one to another; that is, the chairs are drawn into little parties of three together, in a confused manner, all over the room.

The drawing room became more than ever before a place to reflect the taste, and often the income, of the owner. In 1771, at Fawley Court, near Henley, for example, Mrs Lybbe Powys noticed:

> The saloon with light blue and gold cord … a fine chimney piece, two very beautiful marble tables, on each an elegant candlebranch of ormolu; the paper cost fifty guineas! … On the right hand is the drawing-room, fitted up with every possible elegance of the present taste, hung with crimson strip'd damask, on which are to be pictures; a most

beautiful ceiling painted by Wyatt; the doors curiously inlaid, the window-shutters painted in festoons, a sweet chimney-piece, a grate of Tutenar's, cost 100 guineas; two exceedingly large pier glasses, the chairs and confidant sofa in the French taste.

Owing to – or possibly despite – this expenditure, some drawing rooms were extremely pretty. They were often finished in tones of white paint or paper, the drawing room at Hedsor in 1780, for example, had white flock paper and chairs and curtains in a matching lutestring, a light silk.

Such schemes owed much to the French, who by the mid-eighteenth century had made the combination of white with gold *de rigueur* for formal reception rooms. So widespread was this fashion that on a visit to Paris in 1765, Walpole complained how every town house was 'white and gold and looking glass; I never know one from another'.

The eighteenth century is often characterized as a period of elegance and easy charm, the nineteenth one of heaviness and clutter, but change took time. During the early nineteenth century the Classical style swept the drawing rooms of Europe and America. In France furniture designs of the Empire period echoed the Classical connotations, linear sweep and Egyptian and Greek motifs of the English Regency, and the window became an integral part of both styles. Curtains became more elaborate, with light fabrics held back by braid or rope, headed with soft swags or pelmets.

In America, the interest in the Classical form, so popular for both public and domestic architecture, found expression in the Federal style, in furniture designed by such men as Duncan Phyfe of New York and Samuel McIntire of Salem. The American drawing room of the early 1800s was a splendid thing. Thomas Jefferson, the architect–president, made Neoclassicism almost a national style. Now the panelled drawing room was painted and papered, with cornices and chimneypieces just as in Europe. And yet there was an airiness, an elegance and a sense of proportion that owed little or nothing to the old country.

By the 1820s, however, the early Federal style had given way to a more identifiable Neoclassicism peppered with Grecian and Egyptian stylistic detail. Sometimes successful, it had nevertheless a tendency to heaviness, and on the East Coast

The music corner of a drawing room with the musical instruments ready for play. Everything is of the finest quality from the elaborate parquet floor set in a radiating star pattern, to the detail of the swagged, tailed and tied-back curtains.

A fine harpsichord made from different woods, finished in black lacquer, outlined in gold.

some drawing rooms lost their stylish simplicity to become as ornately filled as their European counterparts. In New York at this time, Frances Trollope noticed the similarities:

> Little tables, looking and smelling like flower beds, portfolios, nicknacks, bronzes, busts, cameos, and alabaster vases, illustrated copies of lady-like rhymes bound in silk, and, in short, all the coxcomalities of the drawing room scattered about with the same profuse and studied negligence as with us.

In England, what we now tend to think of as the typical Victorian look was ubiquitous by 1850. The drawing room appeared overcrowded, not necessarily because there were more pieces in it than there had been a century before, but because each piece was more heavily designed, more elaborate, overstuffed. Textiles were everywhere, at the windows in double or even treble thicknesses, and draping the fireplace, tables, piano and even the door. Chairs and sofas were upholstered in deep velvets, dark rep and light-absorbing plush. Over the upholstery went everyday loose covers, and when the room was not in use, there were further layers of brown holland covers. The resultant gloom was increased by the woodwork, which, painted or varnished dark chocolate-brown, did even more to deaden the light.

By the mid-nineteenth century the new mechanized carpet looms – in general use by 1850 – meant that Axminster carpets were more widely affordable, and their decorative possibilities were extended by the fact that they could now be cut in strips to cover the entire floor. Another invention that changed the look of rooms were synthetic dyes. Not only were these new colours considerably brighter than the old vegetable dyes, but they also faded less evenly, with the resultant strange strident contrasts.

Victorian ladies were as fascinated as their predecessors had been with amateur arts and crafts. Their passion for needlework is displayed in the myriad cushions, chairs, footstools, mantelpiece strips and screens they produced. Other artistic ornaments included wax fruits under domes, dried, pressed and shell flowers. Photograph and scrap albums give witness to the thriving print industry, and pokerwork and papier-mâché speak of long, idle hours.

The style for styles affected the Victorian interior from about 1850. The quest for originality meant that any look which could be given a name was enthusiastically accepted. With the Exotic, many a drawing room was filled with the mystery of the East, much of it manufactured in England, but there was also the Renaissance look, a sort of formal Vatican grandeur, as well as Greek and Jacobethan revivals. But the one with the most impact was the Gothic Revival, which was a serious attempt to emulate great medieval architecture, initiated by Augustus Charles Pugin and carried on by his son A. W. N. Pugin until his death in 1852.

If English, and indeed French, drawing rooms reflected this nostalgia for the past, in Austria and Germany what came to be known as Biedermeier style was firmly in vogue during the early to mid-nineteenth century. Unpretentious and unadorned, its domestic modernism predated the move towards the simpler style advocated by William Morris and the English Arts and Craft Movement.

By the 1870s, Morris's domestic designs for wallpapers, textiles and even carpets, as well as his flat, naturalistic patterns, were having a profound effect on domestic decoration. Everything became softer. Fabrics like cotton cretonne were seen in curtains, and for the first time for many years white was seen, both on paintwork – which was considered very modern – and in furnishings. An appreciation of comfort, informality and beauty was emerging.

Books were published on aspects of interior decoration, but unlike the eighteenth-century works of designers and architects, these were by a new breed – interior decorators. And people took notice, as Osbert Sitwell, writing of a move made in 1900, described:

> In the house that we had taken, mauve, I remember, was the colour on which each scheme was founded. Indeed mauve was the acme of fashion in all branches of decoration, whether for ceilings or wallpapers, and for coverings, of a woman herself less than of her furniture.

Suddenly everyone could be his or her own decorator, and the start of the twentieth century saw an eclectic profusion of styles and taste that remains with us today.

A detailed and extraordinary chest of
drawers in marquetry with brass
handles and turned legs.

A grand but comfortable country
drawing room with inviting
armchairs covered in scaled-down
chintz, occasional tables home to
framed family photographs, and a
table in the corner set ready for an
after dinner game of cards.

The formal drawing room in the Georgian House at Hever Castle. The musicians amuse themselves amidst gilded splendour beneath small-scale ancestral portraits. The imposing furniture includes a perfectly reproduced break-front cabinet filled with books and handmade porcelain.

Below: A long view of the same drawing room, clearly showing the perfect proportions and scale of this unusual and astonishing room.

Another view of the stately drawing room at Hever, showing the fine oval mirror of the chimneypiece above the glowing coals and brass fender of the fire. Chinese Chippendale cabinets house some of the collection of fine china.

A detail of the room (left) showing
the fine broken-pediment bookcase,
and the coffee about to be served
from a silver service on the table.
The hand-painted cushions are a fine
detail.

A small, cheerful English drawing
room that combines comfort with
symmetrical beauty. Knole sofas
stand either side of the fire flanked
by a pair of tazzas on side tables.
Two obelisks stand on the
mantelpiece, above which hang long
flower swags. The painting above
the fireplace is balanced by the
bright needlework fire screen.

THE DRAWING ROOM

Furnished with comfortable
Victorian clutter, as well as the odd
good eighteenth-century piece, this
room is made for a life of leisure
from the music on the stand to the
tea and cake ready with the kettle by
the log fire. The whole room is
scented by the bowl of pot pourri on
the piano.

An eighteenth-century style
chest of drawers in veneer with
brass handles.

A drawing room at tea time. Most of the furnishings date from the early Victorian period – but the silver-framed photogrpahs show a modern touch. Both the side table with tea ready to be poured and the low table with its open box of dates mark this as the room of one who likes his culinary comforts.

A simple room in eighteenth-century taste, with a plain wooden floor, a flat-weave rug, miniatures hung on a wide black ribbon, and a three-part frame on a table that holds more miniatures.

A bright country sitting room whose cheerful yellow walls are picked up by the yellow-checked sofa and the realistic narcissi in their porcelain bowl. Next to the bust on the bureau stands a glass dome with wax birds. Decorative touches include two delicate landscapes and a pair of lively Staffordshire figures.

The drawing room of an eighteenth-century Gothick house where the charming windows need no further adornment. This is a room for relaxing with books on the sofa table, blotter and magnifying glass on the desk, and the table set for tea with cups, saucers and silver tea service. There are bowls of flowers on every surface, fine paintings and happy dogs.

THE DINING ROOM

THE ACT OF dining has always been accompanied by a certain amount of ritual. At the communal meals taken in smoky medieval halls, the lord, who sat on a raised dais, was served elaborate dishes with much ceremony and pageantry, as befitted his rank. By the sixteenth century, however, the family no longer ate in the great hall, but in a separate first-floor room, and consequently eventually there arose the need for two dining areas: one formal for banquets and receptions, and a smaller room for everyday dining.

In seventeenth-century France the same pattern was followed: banquets and grand meals were held in the salon, less formal meals in a small eating parlour. The French dining room did not emerge as a separate room until the reign of Louis XV (1715-74), when as court life became less formal, smaller functional rooms became fashionable. In England, the dining room became common during the eighteenth century, although in polite circles it was more usually known as the eating room, the term 'dining room' being considered vulgar. In Italy a separate dining room was not usual until the nineteenth century.

Dining-room utensils also evolved gradually. Instead of plates, the fourteenth-century guest ate from trenchers or flat loaves. He used his fingers too, sometimes with the help of his personal knife. Bread trenchers gave way to wooden spoons and platters, the latter in turn superseded by plates of pewter or tin. The first

A nineteenth-century Swedish dining room decorated in characteristic style with pale tones of white and blue with gilded details. The room is dominated by the faience-tiled stove in the corner, and one wall is hung with finely detailed blue and white plates.

Another view of the Swedish dining room showing the delicate painting on the panelled walls. The window has a typically simple scalloped blind, and candles hang against mirrored sconces.

A reproduction Tudor dining room complete with the heavily carved oak furniture that enjoyed a revival in the Twenties and Thirties. Even the electric iron chandelier, with its candle-type bulbs, is in keeping with the mood.

pottery came from Delft in Holland in the early seventeenth century and was soon copied at Lambeth in London. Like knives, spoons were personal possessions carried by the owner, and were placed face down in order to keep the bowl free from any grease. By the mid-1600s in France, Germany and the Low Countries, the appearance of the table was also more sophisticated. There were linen tablecloths and napkins, often trimmed with lace and set over fine table carpets. Wine was served from ornate ewers and jugs, some of which were covered as a mark of both the wealth of the host and the importance of the guests. Leather wall hangings were also popular at this time, it being known that fabric wall coverings absorbed food smells.

By the late seventeenth century two-tined forks began to be used in England, an idea that, like so many others, came first from the Continent. Paintings of eighteenth-century court dinners in Vienna show two different styles of fork — two-tined to secure the meat, and three-tined to carry the food to the mouth. Pewter dishes were in general use, pottery was seen in some

houses, whilst the rich and noble ate from silver or gilt.

As with so much else in domestic life, dining became an art during the eighteenth century. The work of men such as the two Josiahs — Spode and Wedgwood — meant that china could easily be bought by polite society, and it was collected and used in great quantities. It was not cheap, but it was new, and for a time it quite superseded silver as the fashionable essential for any well-dressed table. In 1727, Mrs Delany sent her sister-in-law some silver saltcellars, and with them a 'pair of China ones, which you may think old fashion, but it is the new mode, and all salt cellars are now made in that manner'. For those who could not afford Mr Wedgwood's wares, there was always earthenware, now to be found in most people's homes.

During the course of the eighteenth century the hour of dinner became progressively later, although country folk still ate earlier than townspeople. By 1750 rural dinner might be taken as early as 2 o'clock, but in London it would be 4 or even 5 o'clock. It was not until the advent in the nineteenth century of

104

first gas and then electric light that the dinner hour moved to the time we know today.

Dining-room furniture also developed in a practical way over the centuries. Medieval dining tables were boards on trestles, not as primitive a form of furniture as it sounds, since their portability allowed for quick and easy restoration of the hall to its normal, busy state. Trestles evolved into long, heavy tables, but by the seventeenth century the focus of the house had shifted from the great hall, and as the new dining parlours were smaller, tables grew smaller too. They were now round or rectangular, with gate legs and integral leaves, whilst in northern Europe – particularly Holland – round and oval tables were general, covered with the ubiquitous table carpet, a linen cloth being added at mealtimes. By the beginning of the eighteenth century, dinner guests no longer sat at one table but at several small ones – a practical idea, as useful for large parties as for small.

As always, life in France was more sophisticated than elsewhere, and eating rooms reflected this. There were a variety of table styles, usually for four, but sometimes only for two, as with the aptly named *table servante*, a small table with one or two shelves beneath that made the presence of intrusive servants unnecessary.

French tables were handsomely dressed, and at Versailles in the middle of the eighteenth century they were laid with cloths of different fabrics, each one appropriate, according to court etiquette, for a particular occasion.

In England, the Georgians seemed fascinated by the design possibilities of the table. As in the drawing room, there were any number of patterns and sizes, including small tripod tables for two people, and round hinged tables that seated between four and six. Gradually the table became longer, the length supported by a series of gate legs. By the second half of the eighteenth century it had evolved into a much more sophisticated piece of furniture, supported by a central pedestal, and often with extra detachable leaves. By now the various reception rooms of a house had very clear functions, and the dining room was strictly for eating. Prior to this there had been no specific designs for dining tables or chairs, but now tables could be designed as permanent pieces of furniture.

The elevation of the dining room coincided with the rise of English cabinet-making and such a fine room inevitably became a showcase for the visible wealth and grandeur of a family, in particular – much as in the medieval dining hall – for any gold or silver plate. This was no longer displayed on the simple cupboard of the fourteenth century, but on the sideboard, which steadily became larger and more elaborate until it was as important an element as the table and chairs. The sideboard also held the wine, which was often kept in specially designed mahogany coolers or cellarets that stood either end of the sideboard. Wine was a serious business and there was much in the way of accessories such as cradles, decanter tilters and canterburies. On some sideboards there would also be a mahogany knife box, inlaid and mounted in silver. Egg cups often had their own sideboard stand, and there were the necessary chamber pots, modestly kept in a side cupboard for the gentlemen's use after dinner.

Dining chairs at the beginning of the eighteenth century were wide-seated to accommodate wide dresses and frock coats. Chairs were ranged against the sides of the room when not in use, indeed the chairs of both Chippendale and Hepplewhite were decorated to be seen only from the front, and in France the new comfortable upholstered chairs were often made without any back cover at all. The French also used comfortable dining-room sofas, and they too stood against the walls when not in use. The relation of chair height to dado rail became all-important, for practical as well as aesthetic reasons: the dado rail prevented the chair from damaging the wall. Robert Adam turned this practical necessity into a decorative advantage by specifying that the dado and chair top be decorated as an entity.

By the end of the eighteenth century dinner had become a truly elegant affair. The trouble to which eighteenth-century party-givers went to give glittering evenings can be seen in contemporary descriptions. Mrs Lybbe Powys describes a supper held in 1777:

> At half an hour after twelve the supper was announced, and the hall doors thrown open, on entering which nothing could have been more striking, as you know 'tis so fine a one and was then illuminated by three hundred colour'd lamps round the six doors, over the chimney and over the statue at the other end. The tables were a long one down the room, terminated by a crescent at each end, and a crescent table against the two doors in

the middle; the windows were sideboards. The tables had a most pleasing effect, ornamented with everything in the confectionary way, and festoons and wreaths of artificial flowers prettily disposed; all fruits of the season, as grapes, pines &c.

By this time the food served at a formal dinner was served rather like a modern buffet, with two or three courses. Unlike today, though, each course was the equivalent of a contemporary lavish meal and included soup, fish, game and meat. Symmetry was vital, and everything would be set on the table at once. At a house with enough servants, the footmen would help each guest, but in a house without a full complement of staff, the guests fended for themselves, either by attracting another diner's attention, or by eating only those dishes within reach. The number of dishes served was always noted – anything over twelve was considered excellent – and the addition of a second soup was considered lavish. Wine stood on the sideboard, from where it was served as required. Drinking glasses in deep colours were now quite usual, but there was as yet only one glass per guest, and this was rinsed in a cistern at the sideboard before being refilled.

After the serving of dinner came the dessert, always a separate course, which consisted of fruits, sweets and wine. In the sixteenth and seventeenth centuries, dessert, otherwise known as a banquet, had not only been a separate course but was often served in a completely different place, sometimes a building constructed for the purpose such as the Banqueting House at Whitehall. By the eighteenth century the remnants of this custom meant that dessert, although taken in the dining room, was presented in the grand manner.

Once cleared of earlier dishes, the table and the sideboard would both be covered with a variety of decorative pieces. There would be an epergne filled with fruits, sweetmeats and sometimes lit with candles. There might be figures and other fantasies, as ornate as the level of skill of the pastry chef and concocted from spun sugar – an Italian tradition. These sugar figures were later replicated in porcelain by Meissen and others. Whether sugar or porcelain, the figures were often grouped together in small scenes. In 1783 Parson Woodforde described such a scene on the table of the Bishop of Norwich:

A most beautiful Artificial Garden in the Center of the Table remained at Dinner and afterwards, it was one of the prettiest things I ever saw, about a Yard long, and about 18 inches wide, in the middle of which was a high round Temple supported on round Pillars, the Pillars were wreathed round with artificial Flowers – on one side was a Shepherdess on the other a Shepherd, several handsome Urns decorated with artificial Flowers also etc.

Other eye-catchers included cream-filled glass pyramids and china pyramid moulds with designs of flowers and butterflies painted in the centre so that they could be seen through the jellies. Indeed, there were as many porcelain and creamware containers for dessert as there were dishes for the main courses.

Dining in early nineteenth-century New York was not conducted in the same manner. Frances Trollope in 1829 felt that not only was the dining ritual inferior to the English model, but also the arrangement of the important reception rooms:

In nearly all the houses the dining and drawing rooms are on the same floor, with ample folding doors between them; when thrown together they certainly make a very noble apartment; but no doors can be barrier sufficient between dining and drawing-rooms. Mixed dinner parties of ladies and gentlemen, however are very rare, which is a great defect in the society.

Richard Rush, the Anglophile American ambassador to London from 1817 to 1825, was fascinated by social detail. In 1819 at the home of Lord Castlereagh, the Foreign Secretary, he noted that the dining room had a portière that was drawn aside as the guests entered, silver everywhere, from plates to wine coolers, and long white cloths draping the polished surface of the long table. Indeed, much thought was given to the look of the table generally, although few went to the lengths of the Prince Regent at his ball in June 1811, when the table allotted to the royal party somehow held a stream complete with swimming fish running its entire length.

By this time, formal London dinners usually consisted of

about twelve to sixteen guests, sometimes less. Dinner was in the early evening and thus candlelight was required. Orderly and beautiful tables were ornamented with large silver or sometimes gold pieces, a fact that always struck foreigners, but which was simply a continuation of the earlier cupboard tradition.

There were other popular forms of decoration too. In the 1800s, Lord Ronald Gower described the ceiling of the Cliveden dining room as 'a series of fruit-covered trellises. So true to nature is the painting of this ceiling that the peaches, grapes, figs, pomegranates seem ready to fall on the floor', and in Lincoln's Inn Fields, Sir John Soane's breakfast room groaned beneath a painted and fruited trellis. Such cornucopian symbols had been popular since ancient Rome, and during the Regency period the formality of the new dining room was emphasized by such delvings into the Classical past. At Carlton House, the future George IV commissioned much furniture in the so-called antique style, the designs based on finds made in contemporary excavations of Classical Greece and Rome.

Whilst the early nineteenth-century dining room still retained this decorative lightness of touch, however, there were also signs of the enquiring and inventive nature so typical of the Victorians of the latter part of the century. During his architectural and horticultural travels, John Claudius Loudon chronicled much of the minutiae of middle-class life, including in 1829 a certain Mr Mangle's dining room, where he found such resourceful ideas as oilcloth-covered slips of lead laid along the carpet at skirting level to prevent the chairs from being pushed too near the wall, and a 'contrivance for receiving the dinner hot straight from the kitchen'. Decoratively, this room still reflected Regency taste, with walls in brown moreen, and doorways and picture frames inlaid and edged in bird's-eye maple.

Thirty years later, the light elegant pedestal table of the Georgian dining room had been replaced by the mid-Victorian version of heavy mahogany, bulky and imposing, with matching chairs, and usually laid with protective baize under the white or ivory damask cloth. Instead of the racehorse-legged sideboard, there might now be one that descended heavily to the floor, or a chiffonier with curved and mirrored back, complete with cupboards and drawers.

During this period a minor revolution arrived in the dining room in the form of service *à la Russe*. Instead of all the dishes being served at once, the food was now served in order from the sideboard by the footman who stood behind each diner. This form of service – which can still be seen at state banquets today – required far more china, glass and cutlery on the table. But there was still room for decoration – particularly in the form of flowers.

Until now flowers had not been used in the dining room, but as the century progressed they became an integral part of table decoration. There was always a centrepiece, usually accompanied by single vases. Early editions of *Mrs Beeton's Household Management* show silver trumpet shapes, filled with arching sprays, set in front of each place setting. Also popular for buffets were floral arches made from climbers such as honeysuckle, vines or ivy, which curved upwards from a base secured at either end of the table. Floral hammocks swung up the table, woven from spring flowers or autumn creepers, and there was even a fashion of using small palms as if they grew from the table itself. The mahogany top was replaced by one of deal and holes were cut through the surface so that the plant in its pot could be lodged beneath. Tablecloths, too, could be decorated with swags and garlands of leaves and smilax, often caught, for good measure, with knots or ribbons of flowers or fabric.

Dinners reached a peak of formality towards the end of the century. Dinner at a ducal house, for example, followed a precise ritualistic pattern, as Diana Cooper described:

> The table was dressed in the most lavish manner: There was the marine service, all crabs and lobsters with Neptune surmounting the shells and tridents … and there was the Charles II oriental silver, and the Charles II gold, and the Charles rose-bowl filled with floating camellias, and for great occasions the Cellini ewer and basin.

An early indication, perhaps, of the way in which the dining room has moved in our own century to become a room where often formality bespoke cheerlessness, and display warmth.

One end of the Georgian dining room at Hever Castle showing the gilded and marbled Corinthian columns framing the alcove. On the fine serpentine sideboard stands an epergne filled with fruit for the dessert course. Oriental porcelain plates decorate the wall behind.

A longer view of the Georgian dining room at Hever Castle. The four-pedestal table is set for twelve, with a bone china service after Wedgwood and silver cutlery and wine coolers. On either side of the chimneypiece stand gilded and marbled tables holding yet more Oriental porcelain. The chandelier is of crystal.

A detail from the dining room
(right) with a glass fruit stand on a
three-tiered whatnot.

A simple but elegant dining room in
eighteenth-century style with a
cabinet on a stand, chairs after a
Chippendale design, a simple
fireplace and uncurtained windows.
A knife box and a bunch of grapes
stand on the sideboard, alongside a
pile of dessert dishes and silver sauce
boats and candlesticks.

The dramatic dining room of Pembroke Palace at Wilton House. It is decorated in the Etruscan style, that was popular in the mid-eighteenth century, at the time of the archaeological discoveries at Herculaneum and Pompeii.

A small and cosy early nineteenth-century family dining room with warm pink walls and rug. An elaborate epergne on the table has cherubs cradling an openwork porcelain bowl. The essential silvered pheasants stand at the side, as do the napkin rings and cigar box, also in silver.

A blue and yellow dining room belonging to a collector of miniature antiques and china. It is an eclectic selection, ranging from the larger blue-and-white pots on top of the corner display cabinets to the smaller hand-painted pieces both inside the cabinets and hung on the walls. An elaborate flower arrangement stands with the candelabra on the table.

A detail of the table. A rich
assortment of silver, glass, china and
flowers are displayed on the table.

A treasure-house of a dining room.
The hand-painted wallpaper is of the
kind exported from China in the
early eighteenth century. Deep red
lacquered furniture, very fashionable
during that period and also originally
imported from the East, is set off by
a pair of heavily gilded slaves.

A warm winter dining room with a
thick rug, rich and heavy curtains, a
fire with its log basket ready beside
it, and an inviting printed tablecloth.

THE DINING ROOM

A small and simple dining room in late Georgian style with the table set for four. Boldly striped walls set off the brass chandelier and matching sconces.

A traditional English dining room that mixes periods and styles. There is a knife box on the sideboard, as well as a blue glass jug and tumblers, and a large bowl of fruit. On the table is a large bowl of roses, silver cutlery and a handbell. Waiting in the Georgian cellaret is the wine, chilling in ice.

A dining room of the 1860s full of fabric, including a velvet curtain over the door and a lace tablecloth and sideboard runner. The room is highly patterned, from the bright design of the carpet to the flowered wallpaper. Naturally, there is also a potted plant.

A simple room with curtains tied back to let in the light. The fire boasts a brass fender and matching coal scuttle, and silver serving dishes and – decanters stand in a silver serving tray.

Overleaf: Dining in the mode of Charles Rennie Mackintosh. All the pieces of miniature furniture are exact replicas of Mackintosh's designs, as is the silver candelabra. The black grid pattern of the high-backed chairs is picked up in the black and white geometrics of the rug.

THE LIBRARY

THE ARRIVAL of the first printing press in the West in the fifteenth century meant a slow but steadily increasing demand for books, both as educational and as recreational tools. The art spread from Germany, with William Caxton, the first English printer, learning to print in Cologne before setting up his press and bookshop in London behind Westminster Abbey.

Initially, of course, books were not housed in specially designed rooms. They were few in number and their rarity value meant that a more appropriate keeping place was under lock and key in a cupboard or chest. By the late seventeenth century, however, more people had private libraries, although few had the quantity of books seen in a contemporary view of Samuel Pepys's collection, with its purpose-built, apparently glazed bookcases. Libraries such as these were strictly for the use of the owner – books were not thought of as available for general consumption. But as more people began to read for pleasure, and the first circulating libraries appeared during the eighteenth century, the idea of a separate, comfortable room for the storage and reading of books became appealing, and by the 1750s a library was considered a necessity for the fashionable gentleman and was included on the plans of many a new house. Nevertheless, it was rarely decorated with as much formality as other, grander reception rooms, and indeed often evolved in piecemeal fashion.

The library was also a room where knowledge from all sorts

The library of a Victorian bibliophile with an inquiring mind. Folios straddle the shelves of the imposing bookcase, a globe on its stand sits in the corner, and the restful colours are conducive to studying. On top of the table are a pipe rack complete with pipes, a magnifying glass for reading the tiniest print, a set of keys and a pencil box full of pencils.

of sources, not just from books, could be pursued. In 1758, Mrs Delany described Lady Rawdon's library in Ireland as:

> delightful, with recesses where you may sit and read books of all kinds to amuse the fancy as well as improve the mind – telescopes, microscopes and all the scientific apparatus; everyone chooses their employments – it is the land of liberty, yet of regularity.

It could also be a room for pleasure, as Mrs Lybbe Powys noted in 1778: 'In this room besides a good collection of books, there is every other kind of amusement, a billiary and other tables, and a few good pictures.' The billiard table had been introduced to this country about a century earlier, and stood in either the hall or the library. Extremely expensive, it was considered a status symbol by the Victorians and as such was housed in state in its own room.

By the nineteenth century the library had definitely become the one room where people could be genuinely comfortable, with the overcrowded Victorian drawing room far too full of bibelots to allow any space for books. The library had the easy chairs, the low tables, the best light, and in many houses it was the room to which people most naturally gravitated.

In some houses such as Whittingehame at Haddington in Scotland, the home of Prime Minister Arthur Balfour (1848-1930), a visitor to the house noted that no-one even used the formal drawing room:

> The library at Whittingehame was the main family sitting room. It was a long room, its ceiling supported at one end by two big scagliola pillars. there were two large fireplaces, with French clocks on their mantelpieces. One of them was the centre of a group of ormolu figures representing Diana the Huntress with her chariot drawn by deer and hounds following in leash.

There were of course two pieces of furniture without which no self-respecting library could be complete: the bookcase and the desk. The desk is a pleasing object. Complete in itself, it is an object of beauty that has a definite purpose. During the

Middle Ages, writing desks were sloping, portable boxes, but over the centuries the desk developed from such simple beginnings into the more elaborate pieces of the late 1700s and early 1800s. One obvious development of the box on a stand was the escritoire of the late seventeenth century. Early fall-fronted

chests were too top-heavy to stand on uncertain legs, and so the chest of drawers underneath was developed. Interiors became more detailed with many small-drawered secret compartments.

During the eighteenth century, as houses grew larger and cabinet makers became more sophisticated and skilled, the escritoire

The elegant library of the Georgian House at Hever Castle, the built-in bookcases hold valuable leather-bound volumes, whilst the wineglass on the desk shows that this is a room for pleasure as well as business.

131

shape developed around 1760 into what became known as the secretaire, a far more elaborate piece of furniture, sometimes curved with pediments and other decoration, and narrow enough to stand between the tall windows of the new houses. The secretaire had a cupboard above a small full-fronted or sloping desk, often with three or four drawers, as well as shelves and pigeonholes for writing equipment such as an inkstand, which was usually set with ink bottles and gleaming brass mounts.

From the mid eighteenth century the desk sometimes appeared as a combined bureau and bookcase, often decorated with Neoclassical ornament. It was made in three parts – base, books and pediment – and veneered in mahogany, although by the nineteenth century such pieces were often made in oak, a wood much admired by the Victorians.

The imposing pedestal desk, also not seen until the middle of the eighteenth century, was developed from bedroom or dressing room furniture. Again made in oak in the nineteenth century, these desks are still part of library furniture today, often in mahogany or baywood covered with a veneer. Writing tables were also popular in the nineteenth century, sometimes a version of the famous Carlton House desk, the back of which was sometimes curved in a D-shape, and sometimes rectangular. Ladies' versions had raised shelves and drawers.

Bookcases as such were rarely made before the eighteenth century when the demand for them became so great that both Chippendale and Sheraton published several pages of designs in their respective directories. Bookbinding was considered an art and fine examples were highly prized, so bookcases, particularly in France, reflected this, with the doors of some fitted with fabric on the inside of the glass to protect the bindings from light.

From the beginning the library was a room in which to display pictures, and many houses had vast quantities of them to show. Pictures had been seen as desirable things to own, both as artistic objects and as records of domestic and national events, since the time of the Tudors, but by the 1700s the craze for collecting them had reached epic proportions. As a result, it was during the eighteenth century that many of today's famous collections were formed and private galleries built to display the works, until by the turn of the nineteenth century it was said that England contained more fine paintings than any other country, with most of them in private houses rather than public galleries or repositories, of which there were still very few.

Copies of paintings were also much in demand, and totally without today's stigma. Portraits, for example, were used in much the same manner as photographs are today. They were seen as mementoes of living or past friends and family, and a copy of a particularly well-liked portrait was a welcome addition to any collection. As far as other pictures were concerned, it was the composition that was important, as opposed to the originality of the work. Copies were made of the great pictures of the day and employed in lavish decorative schemes like that pursued in the 1720s by Henrietta Howard at Marble Hill, where the Great Room was hung with copies of Van Dyck and Rubens.

There were fashions in hanging pictures. At first they were hung simply by knocking the nail directly through the panelling or hangings. During the seventeenth century hanging methods were almost equally haphazard with as many pictures as possible being fitted into the space available. All concepts of proportion and arrangement seem to have been unknown. In Holland and Germany, paintings were usually hung on the small area of wall between the top of the panelling and the ceiling. It was not until the mid-eighteenth century that certain order in the arrangement of pictures came into being. Robert Adam incorporated paintings into the overall scheme of his rooms, and this influenced the hanging of pictures for many years. By the middle of the nineteenth century, however, the cluttered look that had invaded the rest of the house had spread to the walls and again paintings were hung in a seemingly arbitrary fashion.

Of course, paintings were not the only things to be hung on walls. By the eighteenth century printmaking had reached new heights of proficiency, and the popularity of prints was such that one dealer, a Mr Fores, rented them out on a daily basis. They were displayed either mounted on to coarse cloth stretched tightly across a frame, or pasted directly on to the walls of the room. By the 1760s some printmakers were printing sheets of ready-drawn frames, swags, garlands and other ornamental surrounds, all of which could be used with the prints themselves to form a series of designs. From these convenient beginnings arose the highly fashionable print room. At Fawley Court near Henley, the billiard room was decorated in this style. Mrs Lybbe Powys described it thus in 1771:

On the left hand of the saloon is a large billiard room hung with the most beautiful pink India paper, adorned with very good prints, the borders cut out and the ornaments put on with great taste by Broomwich, and the pink colour, besides being uncommon, has a fine effect under prints.

Famous in the nineteenth century were the print rooms at Stratfield Saye, home of the Duke of Wellington. The house contained at least three print rooms, of which only one remains, now restored. Like every fashion, print rooms were not universally admired. Augustus Hare, who saw Stratfield Saye in 1875, more than twenty years after the Duke's death, wrote:

> Most of the bedroom was completely covered with prints pasted on the walls. It was the great Duke's fancy. Some of them are amusing, but the general effect is poor and bad, and the medley curious, especially in some rooms where they were framed in crowds – Lord Eldon, Melancthon, and views of the Alhambra together.

The print room finally fell from favour as a decorative fancy during the nineteenth century with the rise of easily obtainable, brightly patterned wallpapers.

Closets (as they were known in England, cabinets in France and Italy) were small private rooms used as studies or places where valuable or precious collections were kept. Often sumptuously furnished, and decorated with an amazing attention to detail, they can be seen as precursors of the new smaller, more intimate reception rooms. Their reduced size made them ideal showcases for the latest ideas in interior decoration, and they also provided havens from the formality of the drawing room. A typical eighteenth-century decorative fashion that looked its best in such rooms was the Etruscan or Pompeiian style, one of the most charming features of Neoclassical decoration.

Singeries – rooms and furniture painted with images of monkeys dressed in contemporary clothing – enjoyed a brief popularity in England during the eighteenth century. The fashion was imported from France, where two famous examples were the Petit Singerie and the Grand Singerie at Chantilly, executed by Christophe Huet in 1735. Maria Edgeworth saw an example of such decoration in an antechamber at La Celle, once the home of Madame de Pompadour:

> The wainscot is painted in grey with monkeys in men and women's clothes in groups in compartments, the most grotesque figures you can imagine. I have an idea of having read of this cabinet of monkeys, and having heard that the principal monkey who figures in it was some real personage.

Imported to Europe as pets, these monkeys dressed in frilled finery appeared not only on walls but in paintings and on china.

The beauty of some of these smaller reception rooms must have been extraordinary. In 1771, Mrs Lybbe Powys described one such at Mawley; where 'In what is call'd the little drawing room, the wainscot, floor and furniture are inlaid with festoons of flowers in the most curious manner with woods of different colours.' Another functional room that was often decorated with equal care was the music room; where typical decoration might include trophy-like cartouches of musical instruments in plaster, carved wood or painted wall panels.

For those who had not enough room inside to follow their decorative fancies, tented rooms, like small marquees, were occasionally erected outside, to be used when extra reception space was needed. However, few went to such extravagant lengths as John Wilkes, summer resident of the Isle of Wight. In 1792 Mrs Lybbe Powys visited his house, Sandown Cottage near Ryde, and reported:

> The cottage itself has only a few small rooms; but as Mr Wilkes often entertains many families, he has erected in the gardens many of the fashionable canvas ones, fitted up in different manners and of large dimensions. One call'd the Pavilion, another the 'Etruscan', a third a dressing room of Miss Wilkes, others as bedrooms, all very elegantly furnish'd and very clever for summer ... but to those of us who reside so much nearer the Metropolis, the idea of being abroad in such open apartments strikes one with some rather small apprehensions. Some of the rooms contain very capital prints and very fine china.

China, by the mid-eighteenth century, had again become extremely collectable, just as it had been in the seventeenth century when the East India Companies – both Dutch and English –

and the French Compagnie des Indes had imported Chinese porcelain into Europe. The porcelain was often displayed stacked two or three deep on top of the new lacquered cabinets also being imported from the Orient. In Germany, too, porcelain was widely collected, and at the beginning of the eighteenth century Frederick I of Prussia had an entire room for porcelain, which covered every wall.

By the early eighteenth century this Oriental porcelain could be found in England and china collecting became instantly fashionable. By the middle of the century the popularity of the original Eastern pieces had been supplanted by those of European manufacture – from Meissen in Germany, Sèvres in France, and also from English manufactures such as Bow, Derby and Chelsea. Houses great and small had special china display rooms, furnished not only with plates but also jars, pots and plaques.

China collecting again surfaced as a fashionable pastime a century later. Indeed, blue and white china was to be found everywhere as a style of room decoration, from the full dining services on permanent display in large houses to the single, roughly transfer-printed pieces found in cottages, on and around the fireplace, on the walls and propped up against dresser shelves.

During the nineteenth century the morning room was also added to the list of essential reception rooms. It was used at first for female pursuits, in 1840 Augustus Hare recorded that at Buntingsale, near Market Drayton, they still followed the 'Old fashioned custom of all the daughters being expected to spend the whole morning with their mother in the morning room at work around a round table.' Later, reminiscing about the house her parents rented at the turn of the century in Arlington Street, London, Diana Cooper remembered:

> The large morning room had the Kent plasterwork
> of fruit and flowery swags. It was densely packed
> with furniture and loved objects, all of sentiment,
> or things of a colour she could not resist, such as
> blue-green Chinese jars or the dead straw of the
> palm-leaf fan that she used to protect her cheek
> from the fire. A great many of her drawings hung
> on the walls.

The informality of domestic life that these rooms encouraged was instrumental in forming the living rooms of our own time.

A room in the eighteenth-century Nostell Priory baby house, and a fine example of the decorative skills of the day. The walls are decorated with decoupage scenes on a yellow background. Above the imposing chimneypiece a gilded bust is set against grey marble.

Another angle of the print room.
Clearly showing the pheasant urns
and bowl the latter full of geraniums
- the stuffed owl in its case, the
globe and the book on the chair.
Everything here, even the dog,
is at ease.

A print room, made with modern
miniature print-room paper creates a
classic period feel. Each print is
framed and a decorative border runs
around the walls below the cornice.
On the day bed lies an important
parcel, brought in, perhaps by the
owner of the briefcase and stick?

A room in the Nostell Priory baby house. Above the panelling brightly plumaged birds fly through exotic flowers and foliage. On the games table covered with deep pink velvet stand Bristol blue glasses and a decanter. The chimneypiece has a mirrored glass above which hangs a landscape. Oriental porcelain sits on the floor and above the writing bureau.

The collector's room from the eighteenth-century house of Sara Ploos van Amstel. Against this wallpaper of old gold and bright flowers stands a real curiosity cabinet. The drawers are in fact full of a collection of tiny shells.

A music room of great elegance with
gilded and blue-painted panelling
and an ornately decorated ceiling.
A crystal chandelier and a gilded
candelabra light perfect miniature
musical instruments.

A quiet writing room of timeless
charm. There is a comfortable
chintz-covered chair for reading,
watched over by a quartet of exotic
birds, and an elegant table for
writing complete with tiny book
and pencils.

A small Victorian sitting or smoking
room containing comfortable leather
chairs, a round table for reading or
writing, and a faded photograph of
the school team. By the fire is a
wooden coal box.

The study of a Victorian country house. There is evidence of quiet pursuits in the globe and the sewing reel holder. A photograph album lies open, and an Easter egg in its box sits next to Easter daffodils in a pot.

Minute perfection: butterflies displayed in a wall-hung case.

The other side of the country house study. An inkstand and quill pen are on the desk. Above the desk a miniature cabinet stands next to a bowl in which hyacinth bulbs are growing. In a leather chair a copy of the *Financial Times* lies half-read, and by the door a glass-fronted bookcase promises further reading matter.

A warm and cosy gentleman's room,
with a soft red and green decorative
scheme. A violin lies on the floor,
still in its case. A large and
handsome globe stands on the floor
close to the desk, which is
illuminated by a traditonal desk
lamp. The electric lights, combined
with the more traditional elements,
suggest the Edwardian age.

A Victorian study decorated with rich, strong colours and fabrics. The books in the revolving bookcase include *Great Expectations* and above the mantelpiece is a painting of Charles Dickens. A collection of cranberry glass is in the corner, with a cranberry-glass basket on the table. The footstool is upholstered in beadwork, and a box of cigars waits on the small table.

A modern study furnished with old
pieces, including library steps and a
lectern holding a weighty tome. As
relaxation after a day's work, the
chess set is laid out ready for a game.

A contemporary businessman's haven with a traditional feel: classic touches include the handsome desk and broken-pediment tallboy, leather-bound books and antique clock.

THE KITCHEN

THE KITCHEN is probably the only room in the modern house in which much of the equipment, albeit now powered by electricity rather than simpler sources, fulfils the same functions as it did six hundred years ago.

Although originally cooking and eating took place in the same space, by the fourteenth century the kitchen was usually located apart from, though still close to the main hall. Food was roasted, boiled or baked on a rather smoky hearth, fires at that time often smoking rather badly, the flues being too wide and the fire area too broad. Some larger kitchens had two or more fireplaces, each one for a different culinary process.

By the end of the seventeenth century the kitchen was placed further from the central block. Food was colder when it arrived at the table, but at least the attendant smells had vanished.

Whilst the layout of the kitchen remained the same for many years, methods of cooking gradually became more sophisticated, if in a somewhat Heath Robinsonish manner. The open fireplace developed into the open range, which was in general use in kitchens by the end of the seventeenth century. At its simplest, the range was an open fire surrounded by flat hob surfaces and trivets that could swing over the flames. For many centuries, boiling was effected suspending a cauldron-shaped pot over the fire first from a chimney hook, crane or bar, later from adjustable pot-hooks. Meat was roasted on a spit, at first turned by a child, and later turned mechanically, usually by a system of

The sort of cluttered friendly kitchen that is a pleasure to sit in. The week's shopping is on the table, whilst on the floor below some baby garden vegetables lie next to an old knife sharpener and between feeding bowls for both dog and cat. A half eaten raised pie sits next to the flour tub. On either side of the hooded range is a fine collection of blue and white serving dishes.

A selection of finely made pewter pieces from the Museum of Childhood, London. The tea kettle, the spoons and the two dishes at the front of the table are particularly finely detailed.

cogs and wheels. Until the end of the eighteenth century, the roasting spit was horizontal, but then the bottlejack – a brass cylinder with a clockwork spring, underneath which the roast was suspended – came into use.

Although open ranges were made until the end of the nineteenth century, the closed range was advocated – in both England and France – from the eighteenth century, and its arrival altered kitchens substantially. The first kitchen ranges had the facility to control the heat. They burnt coal and were not particularly clean, but most things in the average house were rather grubby due to the coal fires that burned in every room. Some ranges had hotplates over the coal burning boiler, with an oven to one side; others had complicated and elaborate systems of trivets and hooks. In France, ranges had several openings for charcoal burners, known as potagers – on which sauces could be simmered and slowly cooked. Thus allowing French *art de cuisine* to develop along ever more sophisticated lines.

Two of the earliest closed ranges were the Patent Range of Thomas Robinson, designed in 1780 and Mrs Raffald's coal range. Perhaps the most influential, however, was known as Rumford's Range, after its inventor, Count Rumford (1753-1814). The Count was actually a naturalized American, Benjamin Thompson, who lived in Munich, where he worked for the public services and made great improvements in care for the poor. His cooking range for communal kitchens not only allowed the controlled use of heat, but also burned an incredibly small amount of fuel. It was said that fourpence halfpenny bought enough fuel to cook a dinner for a thousand people.

Other essential elements of the efficient kitchen were then, much as they are today, a large table for food preparation, wall shelves and a range of various cupboards for storage, some of which were ventilated so that food would remain fresher longer. Many kitchens of large houses also had dole cupboards which opened on to the courtyard. The remains of any meal – the dole – were left in the cupboard to be taken by anyone in need.

Early kitchen floors were a sea of bones, fat and general detritus, all supposed to be absorbed by the rushes, normally used as a floor covering but which actually helped very little. Not until the eighteenth century were floors made of stone or tiles and kept slightly cleaner, although standards of hygiene were still not impressive.

For centuries fire was a real hazard. Travelling with Horace Walpole in 1763, the Reverend William Cole found the following notice in the servants' hall at Burghley, home of the Earl of Exeter.

> Be it remembered, that the porter observes to play the fire engines on or near the eves of every Christmas, Lady Day, Midsummer and Michaelmas, and at the same time he is to be assisted by as many of the livery servants as are necessary for the due performance of the same, in order to improve and make themselves useful should ourselves or neighbours be visited by that most dreadful calamity, fire.

Although it is often thought that the early diet was very high in meats and low in fresh vegetables, this was not the case in medieval times, or indeed, as late as the sixteenth century. By the seventeenth century, root vegetables such as turnips, parsnips and kohlrabi were all being cultivated. Also grown were globe artichokes, peas, lentils, broad, French and runner beans, pumpkins, asparagus, Swiss chard, mushrooms and even aubergines, recently arrived from Italy and known as madde apples.

Salad stuffs were popular and those grown included several different types of lettuces, chicory, endive, fennel, cucumber and radishes. These could be served with a dressing, sometimes of oil and vinegar, sometimes more elaborate, like the one John Evelyn described in 1699 which consisted not simply of oil and vinegar, but also of lemon peel, horseradish, red pepper and egg yolk.

It appears that whilst a greater variety of foodstuffs was found in the kitchen over the next two hundred years, from the eighteenth century salads and other more perishable vegetables were not as popular as before. Taking their place were quantities of fish and red and white meat, but available vegetables included potatoes, as well as cabbages and sprouts. Heavy steamed puddings were normal fare, along with game and mutton, sometimes served relatively simply, sometimes in elaborate pies.

In addition to a kitchen, these self-sufficient houses of the eighteenth century also had still rooms for distilling; lockable storerooms, bakeries and larders. As a girl in 1756, Mrs Lybbe Powys wrote of a house in Norfolk where venison, game and in particular the famous 'Norfolk mutton' were hung for at least three weeks and sometimes up to six in the specially designed large larder. Ale, the usual drink of most people – at least until the eighteenth century – was brewed on the premises.

By the end of the eighteenth century only the introduction of the range had made any appreciable difference to the kitchen. Sinks were sometimes made of stone, but more often of heavy earthenware, and the sink water was pumped and collected outside. However, the implements and utensils used to achieve all this good housekeeping were very similar in design to their modern counterparts, obviously a sign of good design, function being form. There were bowls, platters and bins made from wood, pewter, tin and earthenware, and the pestle and mortar was used then, as now, for the pounding and crushing of herbs and spices.

The British countryside was not well served with major roads. The further north one travelled the more difficulties presented themselves; as a result large houses had to be entirely self-sufficient as far as services were concerned. Deer, pigs, cows and sheep were kept and killed when necessary. As late as 1840 Barbara Charlton, who lived in Northumbria, was complaining about the fact that the slaughterhouse was built so near to the main dwelling that all the smells, sights and attendant horrors had to be endured. Thus:

> A little later in the Spring, William, at my suggestion dismantled the slaughterhouse from the entrance of the west avenue to the sawmill among trees and well out of sight of the house. It had always been an unmitigated eyesore, it seemed most disgusting to have a slaughterhouse actually in the grounds and so in evidence ... Everyone concerned was delighted at the idea and how old Mrs Charlton, who had made a small garden on that very side of the house, with a greenhouse up against the back wall of the stable, could endure the proximity of reeking sheepskins and flayed carcasses will always be a marvel.

In the country, clothes and household linens were, naturally, washed at home. The household laundry was a lengthy, almost continuous chore. What with soaking, boiling, washing, drying,

The kitchen in the Medieval House at Hever Castle. A cook makes bread in one of the open fires using a long paddle. Sawdust on the floor absorbs the grease and dirt. At the other end of the kitchen, a servant prepares some of the food that will be taken to the Great Hall. At his feet are baskets of fruit and vegetables.

mangling and finally ironing, the whole process took up to a week. Early laundry maids literally batted the clothes clean with large wooden washing bats and then mangled them through heavy rollers. The clean wash was laid out to dry, and woollens were stretched into shape. Clothes were ironed with difficulty. Eighteenth-century irons were either flat and heated on the range, or hollow with a sliding back panel in which hot metal could be slid, and not much had changed by the nineteenth century.

The laundry itself was in some instances known by the mistress of the house as a place of lax morals rather than of clean clothes. Because it was usually situated a short distance away from the house, often near a road and therefore with access to the local village, laundry maids acquired a possibly undeserved reputation for being – at best – a little fast.

Whilst servants remained both easy to obtain and cheap to maintain, kitchens were never going to be revolutionized, and indeed during the nineteenth century there were few changes other than the introduction of a plethora of new, factory-made gadgets without which no home could be complete. Designed to increase the cleanliness and efficiency of the household, these essential gadgets included the Dalek-shaped Sausage Stuffer, the murderous-looking Beef Shaver and the unfathomable Raisin Seeder, guaranteed to remove Every Seed without Waste. The late twentieth-century kitchen seems a far less interesting place than its nineteenth-century counterpart. A typical kitchen was that of Whitmore Lodge, home of Robert Mangles, and described by the writer and architect J.C. Loudon in 1829:

> The walls lined with Dutch tiles, which being glazed do not retain the dust, and they are always clean. The cook said they rendered the place too hot. Instead of charcoal stoves for compound cookery, one immense cast-iron plate is heated on the principle of a common hot-house flue, by a common coal-fire below. Steaming closet and oven very perfect. Cistern behind the fire, which by communicating pipes heats a bath. Ventilation openings near the door and near the ceiling and through wire grating to exclude flies. In the outhouse there was a knife-cleaning machine, and a wheel brush for brushing shoes and the common description of clothes.

The role of the housekeeper throughout the centuries cannot be overestimated. Her power and authority were, in many households, boundless. *The Complete Servant*, first published in 1825, described her role as superintending the whole of the domestic side of things, looking after furniture linen and groceries, including all dried fruits, condiments, soap, candles and other stores. She was also expected to make all pickles and preserves, and distil spirits, oils, and sometimes even made perfumery and cosmetics for the ladies of the house. In 1825, leisure – for the working classes, at any rate - was considered something to be avoided. Small tasks were the answer and *The Complete Servant* recommends that should the would-be paragon of virtue have any free time on her hands in the evening she should best employ her idle, and potentially wicked, hands by preparing for the future domestic needs of the household – grinding small quantities of spices and bottling them; washing, picking and drying currants; breaking, pounding, rolling and sifting white sugar, or paring and drying the rinds of oranges and lemons. For all this work, the authors suggest that the housekeeper should receive between twenty-five and fifty guineas per year – a sum that appears a bargain then and now.

In large houses the housekeeper had her own room in the kitchen wing, and a description was given in the early nineteenth century of one such room in Arthur Balfour's house, Whittingehame.

> Down the stone stairs, along the long stone-flagged passage smelling of paraffin and boot-polish, where whistling footmen in shirtsleeves popped across. On through the swing door which shut off the still-room and the store-room, a region scented with oranges and oatcakes on the girdle. And so into the fairy's room. People who knew no better called it the housekeeper's room, and its owner, Mrs Anderson.

By the nineteenth century the kitchen of a large house was an extremely busy place. There were meals for the adults, which

An almost timeless country kitchen, small and simple. Still made today, both in miniature and life-size, are the stone sink set on bricks, the blacked cooking range, the copper pots and pans and the Windsor chairs. There is knitting waiting on the seat of the chair.

had to be served in the dining room, as well as for the children, which, depending on their ages, might have to be served in both the schoolroom and the nursery. Meals for the servants, depending on how many there were and their status in the household, might have to be served in the housekeeper's room as well as in the servants' hall.

By the middle of the nineteenth century the male cook – or chef – could be found in many smart kitchens. The ultimate status symbol, he was often French and introduced to the menus of the day more delicate food, particularly sauces. Such delicacy did not extend to the menus below stairs however. Augustus Hare recalled that in his grandparents' rectory in 1840, 'the

This rather spartan pre-electricity kitchen is beautifully detailed. A brick boiler stands beneath a shelf holding a box with brushes and cloths for shoe cleaning. Below hangs a traditional dry mop.

men and the maids had only great bowls of bread and milk; tea and bread and butter were never thought of below the housekeeper's room'.

There were other cooks too, of course. In large houses, the head – male – chef would have other lesser chefs working beneath him as well as assorted women helpers, whilst in less grand establishments the head cook would be a woman working with female kitchen and scullery maids.

In families where there was no housekeeper, the cook would undertake most or all of the housekeeper's duties, as well as take charge of the kitchen maids and scullion or scullery maid if there were any. However, in houses where both housekeeper and cook were kept, rivalries could sometimes emerge, particularly when both parties had been used to directing lesser staff, often leading to eccentric practices. At Crewe Hall, in the 1880s, for example, the housekeeper ruled the five or six housemaids and three still-room maids, whilst the kitchen and scullery were under the control of the cook. The result of this arrangement was that eggs were poached or fried in the kitchen and boiled in the still-room.

Kitchens developed during the present century and particularly after the First World War, when servants were no longer easily obtainable, may be more efficient and hygienic, but surely not nearly so interesting as their predecessors.

On the wooden draining board lie teacups waiting to be put away. Above, a set of blue and white plates sits in a wall-hung wooden drainer.

The linen drying room from the eighteenth-century Dutch house of Sara Ploos van Amstel. Beneath a wooden drying rack, it shows in perfect detail an assortment of baskets, some of which are filled with linen, and on the table a basketwork structure designed to keep the shape of nightcaps whilst they dry.

A wash house containing mangle, tubs and washboard and complete down to the last white linen pillowcase.

An astonishingly detailed outhouse used as a storage and work shed. In perfect miniature are the garden sieve, the sacks of potatoes, the tools on the workbench and the garden shears and coiled rope on the walls.

A cook's kitchen in the country. On the mantelpiece, beside the Staffordshire dogs, are stoneware vats, perhaps containing home-made cider. A brace of pheasants wait to be plucked and cooked, and large sacks of potatoes and sugar sit on the floor.

In miniature, an industrious country kitchen where the pheasants are plucked by hand, the clean clothes hung on the drying rack, the carpets regularly cleaned with the cane beater, and fragile possessions are flicked with the feather duster. A ham in muslin hangs from the ceiling.

A detail of the kitchen above with just-picked vegetables in a basket. Under the sink is a cleaning box with a tin of polish, whilst next to the broom lies the all-important mousetrap.

168

A butler's pantry, part kitchen and part cosy sitting room. In one corner sit the dirty boots and the wherewithal to clean them. On the wall is the telephone, and on the other side of the room is a comfortable woven basket chair by a small table on which stands a pot of hot tea. *Home Sweet Home* is prominent on the wall.

Contrasting styles: the twentieth-century kitchen of an eighteenth-century Gothick house. A collection of copper jelly moulds covers the walls, and another collection of blue and white china fills the shelves of the dresser. A gardening trug with flowerpot and trowel sit on the floor. On the table are two cooked chickens and an apple pie ready to go into the oven. A chair is drawn up close to the range with its simmering copper pans.

A blue and white kitchen designed to be used for eating in. The gate-leg table is of oak, and there are nice decorative touches in the painted chest and the baskets of flowers hanging from the ceiling. Blue and white plates decorate the walls, and the parrot's plumage co-ordinates with the whole perfectly.

Beautifully turned country Windsor chairs, one for a miniature adult, the other to hold a diminutive child.

The epitome of the farmhouse kitchen, but with all the comforts of town. The dresser is painted in fashionable soft tones, and the pine table is loaded with food. Conveniences include a kitchen towel on the wall, as well as buckets, broom and cleaning materials, some of which will doubtless be needed to clear up the spilt milk before the cat does.

A breakfast of sausage and eggs cooks on the range of the kitchen, flanked by jars of jam and preserved fruits. A steel hod, a shovel beside it, contains fuel for the range.

THE BEDROOM

THE BEDROOM has always been not only a place of comfort and privacy, but once was also one of status, wealth and power. The bed itself was for a long time the most important piece of furniture in the house, to be bequeathed in wills, listed in inventories and dressed with valuable damask or tapestry hangings.

Although early beds, which stood in an alcove or solar off the Great Hall, were simple affairs consisting of a thin mattress over wooden boards, by the fourteenth century bedrooms were separate and styles of European beds various. Some stood beneath draped testers or under a suspended canopy. Others were backed with draped fabric or simple wooden bedheads. The most sumptuous of all were Italian, decoratively painted and hung with silk velvet. Gradually beds became larger until by the end of the sixteenth century they overpowered everything else. Bed hangings were heavy and draught resistant, with floor-length curtains dropping from a carved and decorated wooden tester.

During the seventeenth century, the box bed became popular in France, Germany, Holland and England. A deep pelmet fitted the frame closely, and the curtains fell straight to the ground, giving a rectangular box look. Hangings were still extremely valuable, even when simple in style. Mattresses were made with a range of fillings, from the simplicity of beech leaves to flock and carded wool and the luxury of swan's down.

In Germany and Holland at this time, the bedchamber was far

A simple but comfortable gentleman's country bedroom of the early Victorian period. The four-poster – without an elaborate set of curtains – is made up with fresh lace-edged white sheets, and matching bolster. On the bed, covered with a red-stitched blanket, a newly laundered coverlet waits to be put on. Underneath the bed is a chamber pot. The blue and white of the finely worked rug are picked up in the colour of the walls and the day bed. A cheval mirror sits in one corner; in the other a washstand with recessed basin and jug beneath.

A detailed look at the same bedroom. Four laundered and pressed shirts lie ready to be put away in the chest of drawers, on top of which sits an ivory brush set.

from being a one-purpose room. Contemporary paintings show the room's owners seated with visitors, the closed drapes of the bed visible in the background. In Germany the bed, probably a four-poster, occupied a section of the room, the rest furnished as a comfortable living room; in Holland there might be a box bed in one corner, surmounted by a shelf cornice and dressed with curtains and a pelmet. As in France, the remaining upholstery would probably be designed to match. Table carpets might also be a feature, whether a traditional Persian weave or a length of rare fabric. Both were extremely valuable and safer on a table than on the floor.

In France the bedroom developed differently from its English counterpart. Whereas in England by the mid-seventeenth century the Great Chamber had usually spawned a second, smaller sleeping room, the French *chambre* remained an all-purpose room used for sleeping, eating and the reception of visitors, with the bed set in an alcove.

It was during the seventeenth century that the state bedroom emerged throughout Europe as a potent symbol of position. Far more than just a richly appointed room, the magnificence of the furnishings and bed told much about the owner's social standing. In both England and France, such a room was envisaged as the triumphant finale of a series of state reception rooms, and was not used for everyday living. Real life took place in a second set of rooms, smaller and more intimate. Some great houses furnished a kingly state bedroom, indicating that they expected to receive a scion of a royal house. In smaller houses, the state bedroom might be furnished richly enough to receive a guest of the rank of marquess or earl. Successive generations added their own state beds in honour of the reigning monarch. At Knole, Fanny Burney reported that one 'Earle of Dorsete' had furnished a state room for James I, whilst a later Earl had dressed another room for James II.

Houses could be thrown into some disarray by the lack of a suitable state bed. Writing in 1778, Lady Louisa Stuart described the agitation felt by the Earl and Countess of Pembroke when a visit to their seat, Wilton, was proposed by King George III and Queen Charlotte. They no longer had a state bed in the state bedroom, which at the time was hung with red damask. However, the resourceful Lord Pembroke managed to hire in Salisbury an appropriately dressed bed, albeit one hung in green. Honour was satisfied even if the colours clashed.

Designs for state beds were published in France and Holland, and one of the most important showed the work of the Huguenot designer Daniel Marot, who was successful in Paris until 1684 when religious persecution forced him to flee to Holland and the court of the future William III. From there, Marot did much to influence contemporary furnishings. His beds had carved cornices and canopies, with hangings that ruched, draped, flowed and rippled, the final designs often more like phantasmagorical ships of the night rather than mere beds.

French bedrooms were far more comfortable than English ones, and by the eighteenth century had a feminine air, becoming almost bedsitting rooms, the hub of domestic life, where guests were entertained during the day. There were by now many alternatives to the traditional four-poster. The bed might be in a niche or alcove, draped with curtains; it might be set sideways to the wall with a narrow centrally hung canopy, or positioned traditionally but hung with a new elegance. Styles ranged from the *lit à l'ange,* in which the canopy was slightly less than the bed length, and the *lit à la duchesse,* where the canopy extended the full length of the bed, to the *lit à la polonaise,* where the canopy fell from a central dome. Decorative ideas flourished, and by the end of the century French bed hangings were often nothing short of fantastic. In the upholsterer's hands they became a cascade of fabric and frippery. Even on traditionally dressed beds, hangings rarely fell straight to the floor. They might be caught with ribbons or looped back with braid and fringing, and were draped and ruched wherever an unadorned corner could be found.

In both Holland and France, the bedroom had become a place for sophisticated unified schemes, where all the furnishings – bed and wall hangings, chairs and stools – were upholstered to match. At the same time in England early Georgian beds showed traces of the Palladian architectural influence apparent elsewhere in the Georgian house, and the tester could be embellished with columns and capitals and decorated with Classical motifs. The hangings were lighter, and were now sometimes cut from the fashionable new cotton chintzes.

By the late 1800s, whilst some state beds still remained, in England (but not in France) they were no longer *de rigueur.* In the comparatively informal English polite society of this period such rituals were considered outdated, although in some particularly high circles the concept lingered well into the nineteenth

The solar of John Hodgson's late Medieval House at Hever Castle, where the lady of the house sits at the table sewing. The room is lined with linenfold panelling, the window has inset panels of heraldic stained glass, and more glass sits on the table. The floor is covered with a rich rug.

century. Lady Holland, writing to her son in 1828, said scathingly of the Duke of Gloucester's domestic arrangements: 'The Duke of Gloucester from absurd pomp does not allow the Duchess to live on the first floor, in order to have a state bedchamber. The folly of the man, in a London street house. So she lives high up.'

The less formal bedrooms of France were charming. Woodwork on walls and bed was often painted in a combination of soft, light colours, perhaps blue or green with white, pink with green, or even yellow and silver. English bedrooms were also pretty, hung with the new wallpapers and draped with light bright fabrics. Describing Fawley Court near Henley, Mrs Lybbe Powys wrote that: 'The next bedchamber is furnish'd with one of the finest red-grounded chintz I ever saw, the panels of the room painted, in each a different Chinese figure larger than life.' Whilst at another country house, Mawley, she noted that 'Lady Blount has more chintz counterpanes than in one house I ever saw; not one bed without very fine ones.'

At the height of the Rococo fashion for chinoiserie many bedrooms were given the full treatment, and in 1760 Mrs Lybbe Powys remarked that at Eastbury in Dorset there was a 'Chinese bedroom and dressing-room in the attic storey, excessively droll and pretty, furnish'd exactly as in China, the bed of an uncommon size, seven feet wide by six long'.

Since the seventeenth century the number of companion rooms belonging to the bedchamber had increased, particularly in France where the formality of aristocratic life led to a desire for some degree of domestic privacy. Even that prince of formality Louis XIV had felt the need for small private rooms or cabinets as they were called in France, and Madame de Pompadour, mistress of his successor, Louis XV, added to one of her country houses, La Celle, an absolute warren of small rooms. By the middle of the eighteenth century, the dressing room had become an essential part of the bedroom in both England and France, a private and pretty place where bibelots of value and beauty, pictures and trinkets could all be displayed. This was the room where imagination and elegance vied for attention. In 1778, for example, for her dressing room in Middleton Park, Lady Jersey had full length shutters made from mirrored glass, which reflected 'the prospect very pleasingly'.

By now, those wallpapers known as Indian were highly fashionable and both Lady Blount at Mawley and Mrs Freeman at Fawley Court, followed the style. Seeing both houses in 1771, Mrs Lybbe Powys admired Lady Blount's dressing room with its: 'fine India paper on pea-green', whilst of Fawley Court she wrote: 'One of the dressing rooms … is prettier than 'tis possible to imagine, the most curious India paper as birds, flowers &c., put up as different pictures in frames of the same, with festoons, India baskets, figures &c on a pea-green paper'. This last description sounds as though the wallpaper pieces had been cut out and used as appliqués in print-room fashion.

Privacy was important. In 1782, Lady Carlow described her own dream dressing room:

> I am going to do up a small room above stairs for my sanctum sanctorum, in which I have everything to myself, and retire to it to paint, read or write, let who will be in the house. In the first place I had it painted, part of which I was obliged to do myself, and I have got a very pretty white spotted paper with a glazed ground for fourpence a yard and a festoon of roses in orange colour and green to go round the top, with a border of some of Adam's patterns to go down the seams.

In early bedchambers extra furniture had been scarce – a chest, a stool and possibly a simple chair, but the mid-eighteenth century brought all manner of new necessities. Across Europe, both men and women required dressing tables, the toilettes of men taking almost as long as those of their wives. Usually rectangular in shape, the tables were sometimes furnished with drawers or a hinged top that opened to reveal storage space. Ladies' dressing tables, whether French, German or English, were remarkably similar: usually a table covered with a deep fabric skirt, and occasionally an overskirt. The mirror was sometimes nonchalantly draped with a scarf or silk shawl.

Toilet equipment varied from the simple to the elaborate. Often made in silver or gold there were innumerable caskets, pots, dishes and bowls, as well as many mirrors, some on pivoting brackets, others free-standing cheval glasses.

Tallboys and chests of drawers were popular as were designs for small tables, including a night table that stood beside the bed. Washstands were designed to hold a china bowl on the upper level and soap below. The eighteenth-century bedroom and dressing room were also home to new, practical inventions specially designed to make daily life more comfortable. There were wig stands of course, complicated shaving mirrors, magnifying lenses, and dressing cases for brushes, bottles, sewing equipment and scissors.

As always, practicality influenced decorative fashion and by the beginning of the nineteenth century heavy hangings were no longer such a necessity as heating became more efficient and rooms more draught-free. Beds might be draped with silk or chintz, often lined with another, lighter fabric and held back with tassels and fringing, not designed to draw at all.

The fully curtained four-poster was now rare, the half-tester more common. For the first time metal instead of wood was used in the design of beds, giving a fragile appearance. These products of the new industrial energy were often coaxed and twisted into shapes that curved upwards, whilst carefully draped fabric fell from coronets, domes and tents, and highlighting fine linen sheets, perhaps edged in lace, fat pillows and bolsters.

By the middle of the nineteenth century, English and French bedrooms and dressing rooms were havens for feminine pursuits, used as much for leisure pursuits such as needlework and reading as for dressing. They were also, like every other room, filled with furniture. The look was cluttered and dark. Windows were half-covered by curtains, wallpaper was densely patterned, and woodwork was painted or varnished in dark colours. As a contrast to the delicately decorated boudoir of a hundred years earlier it is interesting to note the dense layering of an 1870s bedroom in a house lived in by the Sitwell family.

There, the mantelpiece was draped with a central swag, with two rectangular panels of another fabric at either side. A woven rug lay across a circular table, bounded by cretonne-covered chairs and stools, whilst on the floor there was a small patterned rug over a larger carpet. Elaborately designed outer curtains hung over nets, and beyond, flush with the window, hung festoon blinds of lace.

By the end of the nineteenth century however, a lighter touch to interior decoration was apparent throughout Europe. Bedrooms no longer had so much furniture, curtains became less heavy – chintz and cretonne were beginning to be used again – and white paint could now be detected on the woodwork. The dressing table, always prey to excess now sometimes resembled a baby's cot, with ribbons and drapes in muslin and lace, whilst the washstand had developed from a simple corner tripod stand to something like a small sideboard, with a back and often a shelf to hold all the necessary items of a lady's toilette. Beds had lost their canopies and were simple, made from brass, iron or mahogany with the posts dwindling in size to become headboard and footboard. The twentieth century had arrived.

The pink bedroom of the Georgian House at Hever Castle. The simple four-poster, with a Bible lying on it, is dressed in white silk with a deep fringe from the canopy. On the chest is a wig stand. The open linen press is filled with linen. Although the ceiling is of a simple stucco design, the door has an ornate pediment above.

A detail of the same bedroom. The ceramic hip bath with roses splashed across the inside has in it a folded linen towel, and there is a copper pitcher holding the bath's hot water. Pink porcelain on the mantelpiece tones with the pink dressed lady of the portrait.

A bedroom of rosy comfort. The draped four-poster has an elegant sofa in front of it. There is a hip bath, a basin and ewer on the chest, shoes by the fire and flowers on the table.

The writing desk of this well-equipped room, showing a glass paperweight, and envelopes in a pigeon hole. A needlework sampler hangs on the wall.

A detail of the dormered room left, with an immaculate wig on its stand, and an extremely detailed model schooner beside it.

A 1920s Tudor-style bedroom. On the crocheted white coverlet – which matches the edges of the sheets – lie a warming pan and an open stamp album with a magnifying glass. The basin and ewer are of blue and white transfer print.

A young girl's bedroom with twin
brass beds covered in patchwork
quilts. A flowered chintz bedroom
chair stands on a needlepoint carpet,
shielded from the beds by a
Victorian three-part screen. On a
table is a cotton-reel holder and a
pair of photograph frames.

A charming flowered bedroom where columbine climbs over the wardrobe, dressing table, washstand and chest, as well as on the rug and walls. The bed's white linen sheets are trimmed with lace, and both boots and shoes sit on the floor.

THE BEDROOM

A cluttered and friendly children's nursery. The white cupboard is decorated with blue bows, the chest at the back of the room with garlands of flowers. On the floor the Owl and the Pussycat row away from the Noah's Ark above them, towards the comparative safety of the doll's house.

An old-fashioned nursery, with baby's bonnet on the table and a canework cradle at the back of the room. The nursery fire is protected by a fire-guard. Traditional toys include a doll in a high-wheeled pram, a tall doll's house, and a nursery bear on a chair.

A children's room with an exuberant scene of giraffes, lions and monkeys strolling through a jungle mural that covers all the walls. Playthings include a railway set, balloons and a castle and its soldiers.

The bedroom of a hat lover, with one on the sofa and one on a chair. Shoes wait to be put away, a Bible sits on a round table close to a bowl of perfect auriculas. Victorian fashion plates hang over the mantelpiece, with samplers on the other walls.

THE BATHROOM

A bathroom whose green marble bath is copied from the one in Queen Mary's doll's house. All is luxury, from the curved lines of the bath to the double basin with marble splashback and the extravagant dried flower trees in the corners. The bath rack holds soap and a back brush, and a toothbrush stands next to the ewer.

PERSONAL cleanliness has gone through various phases of popularity over the centuries, and it would be a mistake to think that in any particular era people were dirty simply because they did not have either the knowledge or the wherewithal to carry out successful ablutions. The truth is very different: cleanliness, bathing and lavatories were often looked on by many with a certain amount of suspicion.

The Romans, as every schoolchild knows, were very keen on water and cleanliness, villas excavated in Britain still have the remains of intricate underground engineering and plumbing systems. In medieval Europe, too, there was an interest in cleanliness. Communal wooden bathtubs are well documented, stone and metal washstands and basins can be seen in German and English woodcuts, and many castles still have remains of garderobes or privies, which generally emptied directly down a shaft into a cesspit, or indeed straight into the moat.

By the 1500s, however, bathing had fallen into a decline, reviving only slightly in the seventeenth century. Although baths were still not common, at least by this time in both England and France, most bed chambers had a close stool in one of the surrounding closets or cabinets. People kept clean with daily washes performed with a basin and ewer, and pommades and perfumes were used profusely. When baths were required, they were taken in bedrooms, though some large houses did have bathrooms or bathhouses. In 1697, Celia Fiennes described the

A detail of the marble bathroom showing white towels waiting to be used, a backscratcher, and a box holding shaving equipment.

193

The basin shelf in this Edwardian-style bathroom holds a toothbrush and a shaving mirror with magnification.

Marble baths were not for everyone, however. Apart from being extremely expensive, they did not retain heat particularly well, and by the middle of the eighteenth century baths began to be made from various metals, the cheapest in tin, the more expensive in copper.

During the eighteenth century, the French brought to bathing the same sense of style as they gave to everything else. Contemporary pictures and writings show and describe elegant pieces of furniture that often seem more like sofas or chaise longues than simple baths. Also mentioned is the fashion for two baths in one room, one solely for washing, the other for rinsing. And for those without a bathroom, Lawrence Wright in his book *Clean and Decent* describes the work of Paris water-sellers who, up to the nineteenth century, carried hot water and bathtubs through the streets on their carts, carrying both up to customers' apartments on demand.

But whilst not everyone took baths very often, everyone washed, and cabinet-makers produced fine toilet tables and washstands suitable for the dressing rooms of gentlemen.

Water closets, though still not considered the essentials they later became, were also fashionable in London at this time, as Horace Walpole's rather vulgar description in 1760 of those at Miss Chudleigh's house shows:

> I breakfasted the day before yesterday at Aelia Laelia Chudleigh's....of all the curiosities are the CONVENIENCES in every bedchamber: great mahogany projections, as big as her own bubbies, with the holes, brass handles and cocks etc – I could not help saying, it was the LOOSEST family I ever saw. Never was such an intimate union of love and a closestool!

famous bathing room at Chatsworth with its blue and white marble walls, black, red and white marble and stone floor and blue-veined marble bath, which was 'deep as one's middle on the outside and you went down steps into the bath big enough for two people; at the upper end are two Cocks to let in one hot the other cold water to attemper it as persons please. The windows are all private glass.'

The great palaces of France also had magnificent bathrooms. Fontainebleau, the Louvre and, of course, Versailles during the reign of Louis XIV, all boasted veritable temples of marble, gilding and bronze that were designed more to impress than to clean, although it is said that at Versailles there were more than a hundred functional bathrooms. At Versailles too, were a quantity of closestools or chaises percées, often luxuriously covered in velvet and damask, and looking more like thrones than lavatories.

Joseph Bramah patented his famous water closet complete with a system of working valves in 1778, and they were immediately sucessful in the cities. In the country, however, a more usual arrangement was the privy or boghouse at the bottom of the garden usually sited over a cesspit. The contents were generally emptied wherever was easiest, often directly on to the nearest road.

In fact, in such rural areas, even into the nineteenth century people often preferred to use the outside lavatory rather than a more modern one inside. At one house, the new indoor convenience installed in the early 1800s was dismissed as a whim 'such as might breed pestilence and fever'. The shrubbery at the back of the house was the preferred site.

It was the introduction of main drainage during the nineteenth century that finally brought the idea of the bathroom and lavatory into common use, at least in cities in Europe and America. The countryside was still another matter, and even today there remain isolated rural areas where the cesspit reigns smellily supreme. Few places were as up to date as the house in Surrey described in 1829 by the prolific gardener and writer John Loudon. There he found a cistern behind the fire in the kitchen that by 'communicating-pipes heats a bath'. Further north, baths were not generally installed until late in the nineteenth century. At Hesleyside in Northumberland bathtubs were installed in each bedroom by 1850 and this was an innovation, the first time such things had been seen in the county.

The nineteenth century saw for the first time the general acceptance in more modest homes of a room given over as a permanent home for bath and basin. Early nineteenth-century bathrooms were quite low-key affairs, with baths of tinned steel or other metals encased simply in wood. By the end of the century, however, the room could be a grand thing indeed, a testimony to the work of the cabinet-maker, the metal-worker as well as the plumber. Baths were often japanned or lacquered inside and out to represent coloured marble. Feet were plain on those baths designed to be hidden behind panelling, but ornately cast in iron on freestanding baths. This period also saw the invention of those fantastic combination baths with carved mahogany sentry-box showers at one end, offering, through a selection of valves, different water effects, from wave to shower to spray.

Washstands now appeared in the bathroom as well as the bedroom. As monumental and as decoratively profligate as the baths, basins were sometimes encased in wood, but generally were set into a cast-iron frame, as ornate as possible. Tiles were fashionable and were used on floors and walls. The addition of Coal Tar soap in ovals, Brown Windsor soap in squares and pure glycerine soap in tablets ensured total cleanliness.

However, complicated machinery did not mean luxury. The nineteenth-century bathroom was often still cold and cramped.

Diana Cooper, describing the grand town house she and her family occupied at the end of the nineteenth century, wrote that her mother's bathroom, although next door to the bedroom was 'a slip of a bathroom with a narrow tin bath'. On the third floor was 'the special bathroom-cum-box- and lumber-room':

> My father was very pleased. A six-foot-two man, he had never had but a hip-bath and now he could soak at full length and have a very big sponge. I remember how shocked I was when he told me he never used soap in his bath.

And in the late 1800s, the water-men were still employed at Belvoir Castle, as Diana Cooper later recalled:

> The water-men are difficult to believe in today …They were the biggest people I had ever seen … and wore brown clothes, no collars and thick green baize aprons from chin to knee. On their shoulders they carried a wooden yoke from which hung two gigantic cans of water. They moved on a perpetual round. Above the ground floor there was not a drop of hot water and not one bath, so their job was to keep all jugs, cans and kettles full in the bedrooms and morning or evening to bring the hot water for the hip-baths.

When her father became Duke of Rutland, bathrooms were carved out of the deep walls of the castle.

For most people, who were not lucky enough to have their own water-men, the heating of hot water in enormous coppers was one of the first tasks of the kitchen staff every morning. Indeed as with so many inventions of convenience, until the ready supply of cheap servants dried up many households saw no need for plumbing facilities or separate bathrooms as long as servants could be summoned to bring hot water upstairs to a bath that had been cosily and conveniently brought out in one's own bedroom or dressing room and set by a warm fire laid and lit earlier by the same hard-working servant. This was particularly pleasant, because the rest of the house was likely to be at best draughty and at worst extremely cold, as the recollections of a Northumbrian lady show:

During the winter of 1861 we had the hot water pipes laid down in the passages in an effort to warm the house in winter. The mistake was that we did not have the heating systems in the rooms as well, for what could be more dangerous than stepping from a passage at a stove-hot temperature into an icy-cold room; for poor old Wilkinson, who stoked the furnace, had no idea whatever of regulating the heat and under his hands it amounted to a mercy that Hesleyside was not burned to the ground.

In well-run households, the water was heated in large coppers in the kitchen, and the valet's first job every day was to draw and carry up the water for his master's bath, as his counterpart, the lady's maid, did for her mistress. The water was then laboriously taken upstairs to all rooms, including the nursery. Nursery children were washed all over with sponges and water that started warm but quickly became colder. *The Complete Servant*, written in 1825, recommended the following method for gradually making a child hardy:

> Begin with warm water, till by degrees, it will not only bear, but like to be washed with cold. After it is a month old, if it has no cough, fever, nor eruption, the bath should be colder and colder (if the season be mild) and by degrees it may be used as it comes from the spring.

This fascination with the supposed virtues of the cold bath was not new. Athletes had always enjoyed them, and they had been popular during the eighteenth century, when special bathhouses were constructed within the confines of gardens and parks. Sometimes designed to look like ancient grottos, these rooms could be decorated with much elaboration.

Very hot steam or vapour baths were also popular during the nineteenth century, particularly in America which was always open to innovation, ingenuity reached new peaks with the design of baths. The vast distances travelled meant that there was a ready market for portable steam baths, which were available by mail order, usually in cylinder form and constructed from hard-wearing fabric. Fantastical models, both permanent and portable were also patented including one that incorporated a heavily curtained bed with an individual steam boiler and pipe system beneath.

In fact, all manner of designs were patented during this period, including the Sponge Bath (sometimes thoughtfully provided with a fixed stool in the middle), the Slipper Bath, an all-encompassing, shoe-shaped model in which the bather could be assured of total modesty, and the Fountain Bath, a contraption rather like a box over a reversed watering can, which delivered sprays of water upwards when a chain was pulled. Many different styles of travelling baths were also available, complete with lids, locks, straps and handles.

It was from about 1850 that water closets became more general, although in some areas earth closets were preferred, being considered more hygienic than the aqueous variety. With these earth closets, one of which was called Moule's Earth System, dry earth which was carried to the top of the house where it was kept in a type of tank from which it descended through flues to the earth closets on the floors below.

After the fantasies of the late nineteenth century, the introduction of plain white ceramic basins in the early twentieth century with flat tops and room for bottles and soap drastically changed the look of the bathroom. Baths and basins became simpler, and the free-standing shower was introduced. Everything reflected: nickel-plated towel rails and pipes gleamed, whilst floors and walls shone with white tiles, or with the more luxurious but still cold polished marble. The white bath, basin and lavatory twinkled. All very hygienic, but not very welcoming, or even very warm. The ornate, ornamental look of the late Victorian bathroom was gradually replaced by a more austere, less fanciful room, and a style was set that remained throughout the first part of the twentieth century.

A nineteenth-century bathroom with a large porcelain basin on cast-iron brackets. A mahogany towel horse holds thick white towels, and on the floor stands an all-purpose china bucket with lid.

A miniature soap rack hangs over the magnificent wooden bath, which also boasts brass taps.

A miniature bathroom in Edwardian mahogany, from the bath and basin encased in wood to the throne of a lavatory complete with wooden cistern and emergency plunger on the floor. A copper geyser heats the bath, a hot water bottle hangs next to the basin, and a treadle sewing machine has its own corner.

A corner of an old-fashioned country bathroom with a blue and white flowered basin on cast iron brackets, with a shaving stand with mirror. Necessities include bath salts and a box of soaps. Linen towels are hung on a fine-legged towel horse.

The other side of the same bathroom, showing a marble-topped washstand holding a pair of porcelain basins and ewers, an exuberantly floral lavatory complete with chrome piping, a freestanding brass-tapped bath, and charming paintings of the village church and family house.

An early twentieth-century
bathroom with coloured enamel bath
and copper geyser. A sponge bag
hangs by the sturdy basin, and in the
cupboard sit essentials like syrup-of-
figs, soapflakes and toothpaste.
The bath mat next to the scales is
made of cork, as is the lid of the
linen basket. An electric wall-hung
fire warms the room.

BIBLIOGRAPHY

Adams, S & S, *The Complet Servant*, London 1825.

Calvert, Mrs, *An Irish Beauty of the Regency*, London, 1911.

Carberry, Mary, *Happy World, The Story of a Victorian Childhood*, London, 1941.

Charlton, Leo (ed.), *Recollections of a Northumbrian Lady 1815-66,* Jonathan Cape, 1949.

Cooper, Diana, *The Rainbow Comes and Goes*, Hart-Davis, London, 1958.

Creevey, Thomas, *The Creevey Papers*, ed. John Gore, John Murray, London, 1948.

Cullwick, Hannah, *Diaries of Hannah Cullwick, Victorian Maidservant,* ed. Liz Stanley, Virago, London, 1984.

D'Arblay (Fanny Burney), *Diaries and Letters* volumes 1 and 2. Macmillan, London, 1904.

Delany, Mrs, *Autobiography and Correspondence* volumes 2 and 3, ed. Lady Llanover, RichardBentley, London 1861.

Edgeworth, Maria, *Chosen Letters*, Jonathan Cape, London, 1931

Edgeworth, Maria, *Life and Letters,* ed. Augustus Hare, London, 1894.

Gower, Lord Ronald, *Bric-a-Brac*, London, 1888.

Hare, Augustus, Story of My Life, volumes 1 and 3, London, 1896.

Holland, Lady, *The Journal of Elizabeth, Lady Holland 1791-1811,* London, 1908.

Holland, Elizabeth, *Lady Holland to her Son, 1821-1845*, ed. Earl of Ilchester, John Murray, London, 1946.

Leinster, Emily, Duchess of, *Correspondence,* ed. Brian Fitzgerald, volumes 1-3, Stationery Office, Dublin, 1949.

Lieven, Princess, *The Private Letters of Princess Lieven to Prince Metternich 1820-26,* ed P. Quennell, John Murray, London, 1937.

Loudon, J.C., *An Encyclopeadia of Cottage, Family and Villa Architecture,* London, 1833.

Lucy, Mary, Mistress of Chralecote, *Memoirs,* ed. Lady Alice Fairfax-Lucy, Victor Gollancz, London, 1983.

Monkwell, Lady, *A Victorian Diarist,* John Murray, London, 1944.

Powys Lybbe, C, *Diaries of Mrs Lybbe Powys,* ed. Emily J. Climenson, London, 1899.

Quennell, M & C.H.B., *A History of Everyday Things in England,* 4 volumes, Batsford, London, 1947.

Rush, Richard, *A Residence at the Court of London (1817-1825),* Century, London, 1987.

Saint Fond, B.F. de, *Travels in England and Scotland,* Hugh Hopkins, Glasgow, 1907.

Shelley, Lady, *The Diary of Frances, Lady Shelley,* ed. Richard Edgcumbe, London, 1913.

Sitwell, Osbert, *Left Hand, Right Hand,* Macmillan, London, 1945.

Sitwell, Osbert, *Two Generations,* Macmillan, London, 1940.

Stuart, Lady Louisa, *Gleanings from an Old Portfolio*, ed. Mrs Godfrey Clark, David Douglas, 1895.

Taine, Hippolyte, *Notes sur l'Angleterre, 1861*, translation Edward Hyams, London, 1957.

Walpole, Horace, ed. ed. Mrs Paget Toynbee, Oxford, 1903.

Woodford, James, *Diary of a Country Parson,* OUP, London, 1931.

Wright, Lawrence, *Clean and Decent,* Routledge & Kegan Paul, London, 1960.

PICTURE ACKNOWLEDGEMENTS

Gemeentemuseum, The Hague 133, 140-1, 164; Germanische Nationalmuseum, Nuremberg 1; Hever Castle (by kind permission) 36, 44, 65 T, 70, 90, 91; Derry Moore 19-32 (all photographs); Wilton House, Salisbury (by courtesy of the Earl of Pembroke) 107; National Trust 138-9; Ribchester Museum of Childhood 58

LIST OF SOURCES

Most craftspersons or shops listed here produce a catalogue for which a charge is normally made. It is best to enquire in writing, enclosing an A4 self-addressed stamped envelope.

SHOPS: UK

The Singing Tree, 69 New Kings Road, London SW6
071-736 4527
They also offer a large and comprehensive mail order catalogue

The Doll's House, 29 The Market, Covent Garden, London WC2
071-379 7243

Kristin Baybars, 7 Mansfield Road, London NW3
071-267 0934

The Mulberry Bush, 9, George Street, Brighton, West Sussex
0273 493781

Royal Mile Miniatures,
154 Canongate, Royal Mile, Edinburgh, Scotland
031-557 2293

SHOPS: USA

Doll Faire Miniatures,
2310 Monument Blvd., Pleasant Hill, CA 94523
510 680 1993

Minelaine Miniatures
POBox 2062, at the 'Y' Hwy., 179-89A, Sedona, AZ 86336
602 282 2653

Doll House Corner, 8 S.E. Fourth Ave., Delray Beach, FL 33483
407 272 7598

Blackberry Harvest Dollhouse Museum and Shoppe, 18120 Dixie Hwy, Homewood, IL 60430
708 957 4332

Holiday's Doll House Museum and Shop, 7644 W. Touhy, Chicago, IL 60648
312 774 6666

Miniature World & Gifts, 130 5th St., West Des Moines, IA 50265
515 255 5655

Dollhouse Antics, 1343 Madison Ave., New York, NY 10128
212 876 2288

Manhattan Doll House, 176 9th Ave., New York, NY 10011
212 989 5220

Tiny Dollhouse, 1146 Lexington Ave., New York, NY 10021
212 744 3719

DOLL'S HOUSE MAKERS

Kevin Mulvany and Susan Rogers, 2 South Lane, Kingston-upon-Thames, Surrey KT1 2NJ
081-549 2097

Bernardo Traettino, 33 Hertford Avenue, East Sheen, London SW14 8EF
081-878 9055

Reg Miller, 12 Springhurst Road, Shipley, Yorkshire
0274 582537

Pantha at Rosy Duck Designs, 40 Freshfield Street, Brighton BN2 22G
0273 607374

Diminuitive Dwellings, 1 Ty Isaf, Cefn, Gorwydd, Langammarch Wells, Powys LD4 4Dl
0982 552197

Peter Mattinson, 100 Stockton Lane, York YO3 0BU
0904 413236

Lakeland Dolls Houses, 22 Mayo Street, Cockermouth, Cumbria
0900 815777

Architecturally Designed Dollhouses, PO Box 129, Lakeview Drive, North Salem, NY 10560, USA

The Lawbre Company, 888 Tower Road, Unit J, Mundelein, IL 60060, USA

SPECIALIST MINIATURE CABINET MAKERS

John J. Hodgson, 25 Sands Lane, Bridlington, North. Humberside YO15 2JG
0262 674066

Barry Hipwell, 123 Park Road, Loughborough, Leicestershire
0509 215619

John Davenport, 211 Botley Road, Burridge, Hampshire
0489 589767

MINIATURE FURNITURE MAKERS

Charlotte Hunt, 31 Westover Road, London SW18
081-870 3812

Escutcheon, 28 Queslett Road, Streetly, Sutton Coldfield, West Midlands
021-353 5596

Ince to the Foot, 13 Fowlers Close, Little Common, Bexhill-on-Sea, Sussex
0424 846232
Upholstered furniture

Simply Shaker, 86 Oaklands Avenue, Watford, Hertfordshire
0923 226834

Helen O'Keefe, Flat 1, 7 Rosary Gardens, London SW7 4NN
071-370 7659
Painted and decorated furniture

MINIATURE ACCESSORY MAKERS: UK

Gordon Blacklock, 18 Countisbury Road, Norton, Stockton-on-Tees, Cleveland TS20 1PZ
Silver

Jens Torp, PO Box 1035, Pulborough, West Sussex
0798 515034
Silver

Muriel Hopwood, 41 Eastbourne Avenue, Hodge Hill Birmingham B34 6AR
Hand-painted ceramics, including Clarice Cliff

Veronique Cornish, Rose Cottage, The Street, Dilham, nr North Walsham, Norfolk NR28 9PX
Ceramics and pottery, art deco jugs and teapots

Stokesay Ware,, 37 Sandbrook Road, London N16 0SH
071-254 5242
Traditional kitchen stoneware and china

Glassblowing of Greenwich, 324 Creek Road, London SE10
081-853 2248
Decanters, bottles and other glassware

Ann Shepley Ceramic Design, 20 Tilford Road, Farnham , Surrey
0252 722668
Victorian bathroom ceramics and tiles

Terence Stringer, Spindles, Lexham Road, Litcham, Norfolk.
0328 701891
Turned wood

Tim Platt, 62 Great Brockeridge, Bristol BS9 3TZ
0272 629422
Veneered and marquetry boxes

Geoffrey Wonnacott, 12 Ford Crescent, Bradworthy, Holsworthy, Devon EX22 7QR
0409 241705
Detailed and inlaid chess sets, boxes and othersmall pieces

Kenneth Bird, Cherry Hinton, Rectory Road, Deal, Kent
0304 361655
Watercolours of landscapes, seascapes etc

Michael Taylor, Flat 4, 55 Queen's Gardens, London W2 3AF
071-724 5488
Replica oil paintings

Lucy Askew, 5 Sibella Road, London SW4 6JA
071-720 5812
Gilded mirrors and fireplaces

Lilliput Press, 10 Manor Road, Bishopston, Bristol BS7 8PY
0272 248751
Miniature books

Nicola Mascall, The Barn, Whatley Court Yard, Whatley, Nr Frome, Somerset BA11 3LA
0373 836835
Petitpoint samplers, footstools, cushions

Just In Case, 8 Southfields, West Kingsdown, Sevenoaks, Kent
0474 852115
Lined trunks and suitcases

Jonathan Small, Pear Tree Cottage, The Dardy, Nr Crickhowell, Powys
0873 811639
Sporting taxidermy

Sue Austen, Folly End Farm, Ashton, Bishops Waltham, Hampshire SO3 1FQ.
0489 894096
Rocking horses, riding boots and saddlery

Lincoln's of Harrogate, 12 Studley Road, Harrogate, North Yorkshire
0423 507326
Food, including joints of meat and pies

LIST OF SOURCES

MINIATURE ACCESSORY MAKERS: USA

Don Perkins Miniatures, 1708 59th St., Des Moines, IA 50322
Colonial and other period furniture

Nellie Originals, 6001 Edgewater Dr., Corpus Christi, TX 78412
Federal and colonial furniture

Renee Bowen, 28 York St., Kennebunk, ME 04043
Shaker and country furniture

Sir Thomas Thumb, 1398 E. Oregon Rd., Leola, PA 17540
Painted country furniture, garden tools and beehives

Little Things by Jody, PO Box 639, Midvale, UT 84047-0639
Homemade traditional braided rugs

Betty's Wooden Miniatures, Div. Smith Wood Products, 6150 Northwest Hwy, Chicago, IL 60631
Porcelain and tin topped kitchen tables; mailboxes and wind socks; sports equipment
Warling Miniatures, 22453 Covello St., West Hills, CA 91307
Wicker furniture

The Doll's Cobbler, Sylvia Rountree, PO Box 906, Berlin, MD 21811
Leather luggage, boots and fishing tackle

Vernon Pottery, 441 Bethune Dr., Virginia Beach, VA 23452
Salt-glazed stoneware

Barbara Stanton Anderson, 30740 Santana St., Haward, CA 94544
Miniature portraits from photos

Omniarts of Colorado, 498 S. High St., Denver CO 80209
American Indian baskets, pottery and headdresses

DOLL MAKERS

Marie-France Beglan, 41 The Furrows, Walton-on-Thames Surrey
0932 228459

PUBLICATIONS: UK

Dolls House World, Shelley House, 104 High Street, Steyning, West Sussex BN4 3RD
0903 815622

International Dolls' House News, PO Box 79, Southampton, Hampshire SO9 7EZ
0703 771995.

The Home Miniaturist, 22 Churchway, Haddenham, Aylesbury, Bucks HP17 8AA
0844 291419

PUBLICATIONS: USA

Nutshell News, 21027 Crosroads Circle, PO BOx 1612, Waukesha, WI 53187
414 796 8776

Miniatures Showcase, Kalmbach Publishing, PO Box 1612, Waukesha, WI 53187-9950

Miniature Gazette, National Association of Miniature Enthusiasts, 130 N. Rangeline Rd., Carmel, IN 46032

MUSEUMS AND PLACES WHERE DOLLS' HOUSES CAN BE SEEN

UK
Bethnal Green Museum of Childhood, Cambridge Heath Road, London E2
081 980 2415
Part of the Victoria and Albert Museum, with a large collection of dollshouses.

A World in Miniature, North Pier, Oban, Scotland
Open from April to October. Miniatures from some of the finest miniature makers.

Castle Museum, Towe Street, York
0904 53611

The Rotunda Collection, Oxford
Mrs Vivien Greene's collection
Hever Castle, Edenbridge, Kent
John Hodgson's miniatures

Nunnington Hall, Hemsley Yorkshire
The Kitty Carlisle House

American Museum in Britain, Claverton Manor, Nr Bath, Avon

Nostell Priory, Nostell, Nr Wakefild, West Yorkshire
0924 863892
James Paine's Nostell Priory Baby House

Windsor Castle, Windsor, Berkshire
Queen Mary's Doll's House

FRANCE
Chateau Vendeuvre, St Pierre sur Divres, Caen, Normandy

Musée des Arts Decoratifs, Paris

DENMARK
Legoland, Copenhagen

Dansk Folkemuseum, Copenhagen

THE NETHERLANDS
Rijksmuseum, Amsterdam.
Many early houses.

Gemeentemuseum, The Hague
Includes the Sara Ploos van Amstel cabinet

Centraal Museum, Utrecht
Includes the earliest known house

Frans Hals Museum, Haarlam

GERMANY
Castle Museum, Arnstadt
Mon Plaisir

Germanisches Nationalmuseum, Nuremberg

USA
Museum of Miniatures, Santa Monica, California

Petite Elite Museum, 1901 Avenue of the Stars, Suite Los Angeles, California
213 277 8108
Shop as well as museum.

Angels Attic, 516 Colorado Avenue, Santa Monica, CA 90401
213 394 8331

Union County Historical Society Museum, PO Box 35, Blairsville, GA 30512
404 745 5493

The Dollhouse Museum of the Southwest , 2208 Routh Street, Dallas, TX 75201
214 969 5502

The Margaret Strong Museum, One Manhattan Square, Rochester, NY 14607
716 263 2700

The Museums at Stony Brook, 1208 Rt. 25A, Stony Brook, NY 11790
516 751 0066

Washington Doll's House and Toy Museum, 5236 44th St NW, Washington DC 20015
202 244 0024
Includes a shop

The Art Institute of Chicago, Michigan Avenue at Adams St., Chicago, IL 60603
312 443 3500
The Thorne Rooms

Museum of Science and Industry, 57th Street & Lake Shore Drive, Chicago, IL 60637
312 684 1414
Colleen Moore's Castle

The Denver Museum of Miniatures, Dolls and Toys, 1880 Gaylord St., Denver, CO 80206
303 322 3704

Children's Museum of Indianapolis, 3000 N. Meridian, Indianapolis, IN 46206
317 924 5431
Toy and Miniature Museum of Kansas City, 5235 Oak St., Kansas City, MO 64112
816 333 2055

The Children's Museum, 300 Congress St., Museum Wharf, Boston, MA 02210
617 426 6500

Yesteryears Museum, 143 Main St., Sandwich, MA 02563
508 888 2788

The Doll Museum, 520 Thames St., Newport, RI 02840
401 849 0405

Enchanted World Doll Museum, 615 N. Main, Mitchell, SD 57301
605 996 9896

INDEX